CONTEMPORARY PERSPECTIVES *on* LITERACY

Leading
THE NEW LITERACIES

Heidi Hayes Jacobs
SERIES EDITOR

Nitasha CHAUDHURI
Michael L. FISHER
Madeleine Maceda HEIDE
Heidi Hayes JACOBS
Ann Ward JOHNSON
Shabbi LUTHRA
Jane MCGEE
Fiona REYNOLDS
Bill SHESKEY
Jeanne TRIBUZZI
Brandon L. WILEY

Solution Tree | Press

a division of
Solution Tree

555 North Morton Street
Bloomington, IN 47404
800.733.6786 (toll free) / 812.336.7700
FAX: 812.336.7790
email: info@solution-tree.com
solution-tree.com

Visit **go.solution-tree.com/21stcenturyskills** to find direct links to the many tools and resources cited in this book.

Printed in the United States of America

17 16 15 14 13   1 2 3 4 5

FSC
www.fsc.org
MIX
Paper from
responsible sources
FSC® C011935

Library of Congress Cataloging-in-Publication Data

Leading the new literacies / Heidi Hayes Jacobs, series editor [and eleven others].
    pages cm
  Includes bibliographical references and index.
  ISBN 978-1-936764-60-0 (perfect bound) 1. Educational technology--Study and teaching.
2. Technological literacy--Study and teaching. 3. Blended learning. I. Jacobs, Heidi Hayes.
  LB1028.3.L3755 2014
  371.33--dc23
                  2013038888

Solution Tree
Jeffrey C. Jones, CEO
Edmund M. Ackerman, President

Solution Tree Press
President: Douglas M. Rife
Editorial Director: Lesley Bolton
Managing Production Editor: Caroline Weiss
Senior Production Editor: Edward Levy
Copy Editor: Sarah Payne-Mills
Proofreader: Stephanie Koutek
Cover Designer: Jenn Taylor
Text Designer: Laura Kagemann
Text Compositor: Rian Anderson

Acknowledgments

The process of writing a book is both personal and collaborative. Many individuals contributed to the building of this series, bit by bit, page by page, experience by experience. I want to start with a deeply felt thank-you to our chapter authors. Each one of them juggles multiple responsibilities, and I value and appreciate the time and effort each has invested in reflecting on, wrestling with, and defining the new literacies.

In two memorable conversations—one in Melbourne, Australia, and one in San Francisco, California—Douglas Rife, president of Solution Tree Press, prompted me to consider creating the four-book series *Contemporary Perspectives on Literacy*. I am grateful for the personal encouragement and coaching he has provided while concurrently displaying remarkable patience. Outside reviewers, under the direction of Solution Tree Press, gave us solid and incisive feedback on our first drafts that helped our authors rework and craft their text. The editorial staff at Solution Tree Press are of the highest quality, and we continue to appreciate their direction.

Countless numbers of teachers and administrators from around the world work diligently to bring the best to their students every day, and they have provided inspiration for our work at the Curriculum 21 Project. The Curriculum 21 faculty—a group of exceptional professionals—has been supporting educators since the early 2000s. They are an inspiration and a testament to the power of collaboration.

In particular, I want to give a round of applause to Elisa Black and Kathy Scoli for their outstanding and meticulous editorial work preparing chapters for review. Justin Fleisher and Michele Griffin were extremely helpful in assisting me with the research for chapter 4, "Designing a Film Study Curriculum and Canon," in *Mastering Media*

Literacy. Earl Nicholas proved to be a constant anchor and creative soundboard in projects related to merging curriculum and technology.

With constant support and humor, my husband, Jeffrey, is always there for me when I take the plunge into a new project idea. As always, our adult children, Rebecca and Matt, are my ultimate inspiration.

—Heidi Hayes Jacobs, Series Editor

Solution Tree Press would like to thank the following reviewers:

Neelam Chowdhary
Executive Director of Global
  Learning Programs
Asia Society
New York, New York

Christina Conforto
Principal
L. H. Marerro Middle School
Marerro, Louisiana

Paula Eastman
Principal
John T. Waugh Elementary School
Angola, New York

Chic Foote
Director and Senior Consultant
Helix Consulting
Auckland, New Zealand

Barbara Kelley
Senior Consultant
Asia Society
International Studies Schools Network
Raleigh, North Carolina

Anthony Jackson
Vice President of Education
Asia Society
New York, New York

Carol Mendenhall
Director of Coaching
Asia Society
San Antonio, Texas

Honor Moorman
Associate Director of Curriculum
  and Professional Development
Asia Society
New York, New York

Angie Murphy
Principal
Ridgewood High School
New Port Richey, Florida

Lisa Tyrrell
Associate Director, International
  Studies Schools Network
Asia Society
New York, New York

Table of Contents

Chapter 3. Entry Points for Leading and Implementing the New Literacies

By Ann Ward Johnson and Bill Sheskey

Chapter 4. Getting to Superstruct: Continual Transformation of the American School of Bombay 89

By Madeleine Maceda Heide, Fiona Reynolds, Jane McGee, Shabbi Luthra, and Nitasha Chaudhuri

About the Series Editor

Heidi Hayes Jacobs, EdD, is an internationally recognized expert in the fields of curriculum and instruction. She writes and consults on issues and practices pertaining to curriculum mapping, dynamic instruction, and 21st century strategic planning. She is president of Curriculum Designers and director of the Curriculum 21 Project, whose faculty provides professional development services and support to schools and education organizations. Featured prominently as a speaker at conferences, at workshops, and on webinars, Heidi is noted for her engaging, provocative, and forward-thinking presentations. She is an accomplished author, having published eleven books, journal articles, online media, and software platforms. Above all, Heidi views her profession as grounded in a K–12 perspective, thanks to her early years as a high school, middle school, and elementary teacher in Utah, Massachusetts, Connecticut, and New York.

Heidi completed her doctoral work at Columbia University's Teachers College, where she studied under a national Graduate Leadership Fellowship from the U.S. Office of Education. Her master's degree is from the University of Massachusetts at Amherst, and she did her undergraduate studies at the University of Utah. She is married, has two adult children, and lives in Rye, New York.

To learn more about Heidi's work, visit www.curriculum21.com and follow her on Twitter @curriculum21 and @heidihayesjacob. To book Heidi Hayes Jacobs for professional development, contact pd@solution-tree.com.

Introduction

By Heidi Hayes Jacobs

To many of us, the label *21st century* conjures up visions of futuristic scenes from Isaac Asimov's writings. Indeed, labeling global, media, and digital literacies as *21st century skills* is a misnomer. In reality, these are *right now* proficiencies—*new literacies*. Even though the future has caught up with us, and the 21st century is right now, we continue to serve students in school systems that operate on a 19th century timetable and deliver a 20th century curriculum. To reference another futuristic author, our education system functions like a Jules Verne time machine, forcing our students to be time travelers between the present and the past.

Nostalgia for the good old days is pervasive in pockets of society, but it is hard to make a convincing case for going backward in the field of education. In my work with U.S. and international schools, I rarely encounter questions about whether or not we should modernize our education system; the pertinent questions are about *how* we should modernize our education system. Grappling with these questions invariably leads to discussion of three new literacies that exponentially empower us to communicate and create with immediacy: global literacy, media literacy, and digital literacy. The *Contemporary Perspectives on Literacy* four-book series is a place to cultivate the discussion of these new literacies.

There are five primary purposes of the series.

1. To clarify each new literacy in order to provide a basis for curriculum and instructional decision making

2. To find the relationship between traditional print and visual literacy and the three new literacies

3. To provide steps and resources to support the cultivation of each literacy in classrooms and virtual learning environments

4. To identify steps and examples of how to lead the transition from older paradigms to the integration of the three literacies in professional development

5. To inform decision makers on the far-reaching effects of policy and organizational structures on the effective modernization of learning environments

A range of perspectives is essential when examining each literacy and how it interacts with others. To that end, the series includes a cohort of writers from a variety of organizations and disciplines—a classroom teacher, a public school district information technology director, a leadership team from an international school, researchers, university professors, the director of a not-for-profit organization devoted to journalism, the founder of an education network, a media critic, a regional service center professional developer, consultants, the leader of a film- and media-making center, and the director of an international society supporting global learning. This team of authors has come together to share views and experiences with the central goal of expanding and contributing to the practice of educators. The commitment of each author to this work is commendable, and I am grateful for their patience and productivity. Working with them has been a remarkable journey.

In this book series, we consider the distinctive characteristics of each new literacy and how schools can integrate it. The new literacies provide exciting possibilities for classrooms, schools, organizations, and social networks.

This book, *Leading the New Literacies*, begins with my own chapter, "Curricular Intersections of the New Literacies," which examines operational definitions of each literacy and introduces a model for practice in which the intersection of the three literacies leads to digital, media, and global (DMG) project-based learning tasks. This chapter also considers school leaders' mental processes and the actions they must take as they grapple with the three literacies and their implications.

In chapter 2, "Bridging Traditional and Modern Literacy," Jeanne Tribuzzi and Michael L. Fisher show how the new literacies sit on the shoulders of our past work with traditional print literacy.

Administrators and teacher leaders are perplexed about how to cultivate professional development that will encourage faculty members to embrace and employ the new literacies. In chapter 3, "Entry Points for Leading and Implementing the New Literacies," Ann Ward Johnson and Bill Sheskey address this concern. They share a four-phase model for bringing faculty members and school systems into the new century. This chapter includes two unique case studies of schools that have steadily and successfully made the transition to digital, media, and global literacies.

With unrelenting commitment, Madeleine Maceda Heide, Fiona Reynolds, Jane McGee, Shabbi Luthra, and Nitasha Chaudhuri share their journey from a traditional school model to a genuinely contemporary format in chapter 4, "Getting to Superstruct: Continual Transformation of the American School of Bombay." In this chapter, faculty members reflect on their students' progress as they developed the three literacies.

In chapter 5, "Leading for Global Competence: A Schoolwide Approach," Brandon L. Wiley, executive director of the International Studies Schools Network (ISSN), shows how an organizational network can think outside the box and create a consortium model in the great tradition of Ted Sizer. This chapter provides insights on how groups of schools can come together and employ the three literacies to effectively globalize their programs.

We hope that these five chapters will bring different perspectives to the dialogue regarding how to support the shift to new types of learning environments that can integrate digital, media, and global literacy into organizations, teaching practice, administrative styles, and ultimately, the lives of learners.

We encourage you to connect *Leading the New Literacies* with the other three companion books in the series —*Mastering Digital Literacy, Mastering Media Literacy,* and *Mastering Global Literacy*—for a more complete and detailed examination of the new literacies.

Visit **go.solution-tree.com/21stcenturyskills** to access links to the many tools and resources cited in this book.

Heidi Hayes Jacobs, EdD, is an internationally recognized expert in the fields of curriculum and instruction. She writes and consults on issues and practices pertaining to curriculum mapping, dynamic instruction, and 21st century strategic planning. She is president of Curriculum Designers and director of the Curriculum 21 Project, whose faculty provides professional development services and support to schools and education organizations. Featured prominently as a speaker at conferences, at workshops, and on webinars, Heidi is noted for her engaging, provocative, and forward-thinking presentations. She is an accomplished author, having published eleven books, journal articles, online media, and software platforms. Above all, Heidi views her profession as grounded in a K–12 perspective thanks to her early years as a high school, middle school, and elementary teacher in Utah, Massachusetts, Connecticut, and New York.

Heidi completed her doctoral work at Columbia University's Teachers College, where she studied under a national Graduate Leadership Fellowship from the U.S. Office of Education. Her master's degree is from the University of Massachusetts at Amherst, and she did her undergraduate studies at the University of Utah. She is married, has two adult children, and lives in Rye, New York.

To learn more about Heidi's work, visit www.curriculum21.com and follow her on Twitter @curriculum21 and @heidihayesjacob.

To book Heidi Hayes Jacobs for professional development, contact pd@solution -tree.com.

Chapter 1

Curricular Intersections of the New Literacies

By Heidi Hayes Jacobs

The intersection outside Shibuya Station in Tokyo is often considered the world's busiest. Here, eight streets converge, and thousands of people scurry in all directions. Aerial photos of the crossing show continual streams of human beings progressing and intersecting along delineated pathways.

The 21st century is producing educational movement that feels like the intersection outside Shibuya Station. Rapid change and constantly evolving forms of communication make it hard to know where we stand as educators. Digital tools, media access, and global portals create constant motion. We are at a crossroads, confronting decisions about how to cultivate literate learners in these new arenas.

Leaders have a particular challenge. In addition to the endless day-to-day decisions they must make (concerning budgets, schedules, rules, regulations, lunch menus, and building maintenance) and their critical professional responsibilities (supporting students, observing instruction, counseling parents, hiring staff, meeting regulations, and analyzing data), they influence the culture and gestalt of their school. Leaders need to decide in which century their school will function. Daily decisions determine whether a leader is taking students back in time or opening the door to a contemporary learning environment.

Breaking through the barriers of a 19th century schedule with a 20th century curriculum designed for 21st century learners will be inherently uncomfortable. Just because we are used to something does not mean we should be comfortable with it. Education is disruptive.

The contemporary leader models 21st century practices by openly employing the three new literacies: digital, media, and global. Whether you are a teacher leader, principal, school headmaster, department chair, superintendent, professional developer, or student, you have the choice to move forward. This chapter discusses how educators can upgrade curriculum, teaching practices, and learning strategies in order to embrace the three literacies. To set the context for the present, let us first consider the past.

First Forms of Communication

Imagine the beginning of words. Imagine the new feelings and thoughts that human beings had when for the first time sounds emerged with purpose and form, and others understood them. Early language communication emerged from shared utterances through speaking and listening interactions. The beginnings of literacy were a natural outgrowth of time, space, and the need to communicate. As James Paul Gee and Elisabeth Hayes (2011) note, "Language evolved as a capacity in human beings along with the growth of human cultures. We do not know what early stages of human language were like, since there are no early or 'primitive' languages left" (p. 8).

In these earliest humans, the communication dynamic moved from speech to the creation of representative images and symbols. Dating back 40,800 years on the walls of El Castillo, a cave in northern Spain, are the earliest human drawings, which consist of crimson red dots and hand stencils. The images suggest that Neanderthals were our first cave-painters (Than, 2012). Roughly five thousand years later, around 35,000 BCE, in the Chauvet Cave of southern France, we find the stunning and iconic images of large mammals etched into the walls. These are our first media—evidence of the need to share information and give form to meaning.

It has been and continues to be part of our nature to find tools to share the human experience. In our own time, learners must master new literacies and the tools that support them.

Four Points of Intersection

If we step back and look at the contemporary classroom as cultural anthropologists, it is obvious that the exposure to multiple media formats has shifted learning to visual modalities, audio soundtracks, and animated imagery. Communication between individuals and groups is immediate, ranging from FaceTime on cell phones worldwide to Twitter feeds. It is easy for contemporary teachers to be swept up in the tidal wave of new technologies, and we run the risk of employing these new tools and literacies in a piecemeal, halfhearted manner. A teacher might, for example, include the random use of a digital tool as an afterthought or apply the new literacies to dated content and, perhaps unwittingly, hold learners back from investigating the most pressing issues of modern life.

I suggest we take a deep breath and a deeper look at these new literacies, at the way they naturally overlap, and most importantly, at how educators can implement them in sophisticated curriculum and assessment project designs. Educational leadership should be in the forefront of this effort, modeling the intersection of digital, media, and global literacies. To that end, let us look at the following four areas of intersection of the new literacies:

1. **Working definitions**—Integrating the three literacies in the learning environment

2. **Genre fusions**—Connecting the new literacies with classical literacy

3. **Curriculum intersections**—Using digital, media, and global (DMG) projects

4. **Leader actions**—Modeling the new literacies

Working Definitions

In order to make fitting choices for specific learning environments, we need to create teacher- and student-friendly definitions for each form of literacy.

Digital Literacy

The term *digital literacy* has two root words: *digit* (we call numbers *digits*) and *literate*, which means to make meaning. I'd like to suggest a definition for digital literacy based on these root words: the proficiency to effectively employ web 2.0 applications, Internet-based tools, and repository sites to further meaningful research and development; thus, digital literacy requires the following four specific proficiency sets:

1. **Access capability**—Finding resources via keyboarding, voice, and touch technologies

2. **Selection capability**—Strategically locating the appropriate application, tool, or website to match the problem at hand

3. **Curation capability**—Tagging and organizing source material for efficient reference, as in a personal clearinghouse of sources

4. **Creation capability**—Rendering new solutions and forms as seen in an original app design or new software platform

The volume in this series titled *Mastering Digital Literacy* details how teachers and leaders can actively use these four teachable and learnable skill sets in curriculum design and instructional planning.

Media Literacy

Media "mediates" experience. For thousands of years, educators have been helping students interpret written, carved, painted, spoken, and dramatized forms of communication. A scrap of paper may be the vehicle between a poet expressing his feelings and a reader reflecting on the meaning of the poet's words. Anyone reading this page has been exposed to 20th century media, such as film and television, and has experienced images in motion from childhood. Yet it is startling to see the minimal—even tangential—attention given to contemporary media in our schools.

Movie theaters are iterative of the ancient Greek amphitheater, in which audiences sat enthralled with a new form of communication and identified with the chorus. At the cinema, we sit with strangers and watch a story unfold in a rectangular space. That experience has now been transferred to home theaters. Families sit together in front of a big screen and experience past narratives as well as events unfolding in real time. Yet, with all that has transpired through the 20th century and become a seamless part of our way of life, it is surprising that there is so little consistent and deliberate attention in our educational curriculum and standards given to detailed and careful study of new media.

Two types of media literacy, *receptive* and *generative*, are fundamental, and educators can apply each to both the classical and new forms of media.

Receptive Media Literacy

Receptive literacy applies to critical analyses of information and storytelling media modalities. If the media content is informational in nature, students should be able to identify the validity of the source material and the perspective of the presentation. With all content in film, video, and television media, perspective is particularly relevant, since there is literally an *angle*: the way someone holds the camera determines what the learner sees. Similarly, the framing of the camera shot limits what we are exposed to, just as word choice does in a book. We want our learners to be thoughtful about the selection of the words, music, mood, and sounds that are part of a media composition.

With the increased use of computers, tablets, and smartphones, we are consuming information presented on television and in film at unprecedented levels. Receptive media literacy requires students to be astute critics of the media to which they are exposed.

Generative Media Literacy

Generative media literacy refers to students' ability to use media to express informational and narrative perspectives. Generative media skills focus on how to create quality films, podcasts, visual stills, YouTube videos, teleplays, and multimedia products. All of these options for expression are available to students when they have the technical expertise and artistic craft unique to each media genre. Since most teachers have not had formal training in how to make a film or create a professional podcast, we shy away from assigning these types of projects to our students. Educators may have good intentions for generating media-savvy learners, but too frequently the results tend to be superficial. Simply employing a digital camera or using iMovie from an iPad does not ensure quality. As a profession, we need to generate media that support our work, so that we can assist our learners. Reinforcing this focus, Stephen Apkon (2013) notes that "being able to assess and create literate works of filmic art, especially in this new century of visual communication, has educational value in and of itself—a critical life skill" (p. 231).

Global Literacy

Global literacy is a student's ability to connect people, places, problems, and possibilities. Classrooms can make these connections through the use of geographical search tools and through the remarkable opportunity students have to virtually meet others around the world using tools such as Skype, ooVoo, and Google Hangouts. In conjunction with the applications, however, global literacy requires content knowledge. Whatever tools he or she uses, the learner needs to acquire background knowledge about the planet itself, in addition to teaching our students how to find locations and appreciate the role of resources and the juxtaposition of place and politics,

Defining global competencies in action is central to global literacy. Veronica Boix Mansilla and Anthony W. Jackson address this in depth in their chapter "Educating for Global Competence: Redefining Learning for an Interconnected World" in *Mastering Global Literacy*. Their work is predicated on the global competency framework and its four fundamental competencies: (1) investigate the world, (2) recognize perspectives, (3) communicate ideas, and (4) take action (Mansilla & Jackson, 2011). (For a brief discussion of the four competencies, see page 124 and also figure 5.1 on page 136 of this volume.) Supporting these competencies requires content adjustments, and here, I would argue, the prefix *geo* proves useful. *Geo* becomes a curriculum turnkey when attached to the full array of subjects in the curriculum: for example, geoliterature, geopolitics, geo-economics, and geo-arts. Thus, the globally literate student is led to study contemporary interdisciplinary issues.

In order to get a pedagogical handle on the literacies, we have created working definitions that have specific application to classroom life. Why working definitions? Because the new literacies are reshaping not only how we think about teaching and learning but also how we act. They require teachers to integrate them directly into curriculum plans in ways that match the needs of the 21st century learner. When a third-grade teacher designs a unit on marsupials in which her learners will use digital tools to develop a blog in response to a Discovery Channel video and then Skype with a class in Brisbane, Australia, that teacher is creating a new curriculum experience.

Some might argue that, despite the available technology, learning has not altered. They may claim that the human experience has always been about trial and error, acquiring new knowledge, and processing it through human reasoning. There is certainly truth here. However, context determines what students can learn. Digital tools, media access, and global exposure all have an impact on the information delivered to the student and how that student shares the information and with whom. The new literacies have transformed learning. They have transformed social communities and expanded the number of ways we can respond. Does this mean we must cut all ties with time-honored teaching methodologies? Or can we fuse classical teaching techniques and technology?

Genre Fusions

Gutenberg changed information processing with the development of the printing press around the year 1450. Fifteenth-century scholars gained an expanded perspective through print. Not only was a wide range of points of view suddenly accessible through books, there was a new community of readers to extend these ideas and stimulate thought.

Now, over five hundred years later, a student can immediately access multiple sources, images, perspectives, and individuals on a global scale. Not only has the context for study broadened but it is always *in motion*. Books are electronic, and knowledge is constantly updated and replaced with new precepts and information. This creates a pedagogical challenge. How does a teacher determine the background or context for learning? It is well and good that a student can immediately access information about ancient Egypt, but if that student possesses no background information about northern Africa, the Mediterranean, the Nile, or early civilization in general, there is no conceptual hook to hang the information on. Since we do not want to throw out the great traditions of print literacy with the new century's bathwater, it is reasonable to ask, How might we merge the lessons we have learned supporting traditionally literate learners with approaches to the new literacies?

On a practical level, I propose creating classical fusions with our new literacies—that is, intersecting classical print forms and new digital methods of informational delivery. Let us consider, for example, familiar and traditional writing formats.

- Informative

- Persuasive

- Narrative

All teachers recognize these formats and the properties of each. They are old standbys: the informative report, persuasive essay, and narrative story. The key is to fuse them effectively with new digital tools, thus creating a new genre. Before providing examples of these fused genres, a refresher on each of these traditional forms can help guide the process.

- **The informative report** is a significant traditional assignment type. We ask students throughout their school careers to show what they know through reports and displays. A set of synonyms sheds light on the term *informative*: *advisory, communicative, descriptive, edificatory,* and *elucidative*.

- **The persuasive essay** utilizes thoughtful and powerful reasoning to encourage others to believe in or act on specific points of view. The writer employs convincing techniques—whether written, spoken, or visual—to sway the audience. Synonyms for *persuasive* are *compelling, convincing, influential, authoritative,* and *important.*

- **The narrative story** supports storytelling, as the author shares either a real or imagined sequence of events in specific situations, with characters, plot, and setting interwoven to create a coherent experience. The classic form of teaching narrative writing or speaking includes an emphasis on figurative language, thoughtful plot structures, and selection of details to engage the reader. Synonyms for *narrative* are *plot, storyline, recitation,* and *tale.*

Twenty-first-century teaching occurs when we apply these classical formats to new technologies, media, or methods of delivery. We can take the best of the traditional and marry it with a futuristic form, like the third-grade unit on marsupials. Another example would be a fifth-grade class that is studying a Going Green unit making a videocast for the entire school community in which the students act as investigative reporters and explore ways to protect the school environment and avoid waste. Or high school oceanography students might Skype with the director of a major oceanographic research center in Woods Hole, Massachusetts. And to anyone with access to the Internet, the Khan Academy's (www.khanacademy.org) expansive online library of video lectures, tutorials, and activities covering K–12 content areas is available.

A particularly clever use of Twitter as a narrative tool is a six-year project to tweet the events of World War II (https://twitter.com/RealTimeWWII). Oxford history graduate Alwyn Collinson developed the Twitter feed, which recounts the war as if Twitter had existed during the late 1930s and 1940s using various points of view and attached primary-source documents.

This fusion of old-school form with modern function avoids the needless and hubristic battle between the forces of classical teaching and the new genres. In terms of work in the United States, it is noteworthy that the Common Core State Standards for English language arts deliberately set out to include the study of both classical works and new forms of literacy. The description of students meeting the standards is explicit:

> They habitually perform the critical reading necessary to pick carefully through the staggering amount of information available today in print and digitally. They actively seek the wide, deep, and thoughtful engagement with high-quality literary and informational texts that builds knowledge, enlarges experience, and broadens worldviews. (NGA & CCSSO, 2010, p. 3)

The curricular marriage between the best qualities of both can lead to the creation of quality student products and performances.

Curriculum Intersections

Either alone or in combination, the new literacies can live and breathe within the curriculum in the composition of units, courses, and learning experiences. Whether the act of learning takes the form of projects, assignments, performance tasks, events, or activities, these curricular intersections are natural points of integration. Decisions on how to integrate digital, media, and global literacy should be based on what will best serve the needs of learners and support the specific topic or problem they are investigating.

In curriculum design, useful models of practice can help a teacher shape more productive and engaging classroom activity and raise pedagogical consciousness. Specifically, I propose a curricular model based on the concept of the *portal*—a learning experience with no specific beginning or entry point. Here, the point of origin and sequence are less important than the outcome. For example, if an architect is conceiving a building, the initial inspiration might come from available materials or a unique feature that he or she wishes to bring to the design, or the architect may have an overall vision of the style of the building. The design's point of origin is not critical. The sequence of actions follows naturally and logically, and all of the elements—from style to proportion and materials—come together in the blueprint. Ultimately, all the structural decisions the architect makes will also need to align with deadlines, zoning standards, and budgets. Similarly, the entry point for revising or creating a curriculum can be through the portal of the basic curriculum elements of content, skill, or assessment, but ultimately the three literacies will upgrade these elements at the critical point of intersection: the DMG project.

The portal model is flexible. Curriculum models that are too rigid and sequential at the outset result in inflexible, linear plans. Given the natural fluidity of the three literacies, our models for practice should also have flexible characteristics.

Consider figure 1.1, showing the point of intersection of digital, media, and global projects. At the point of intersection, we can develop rich, dynamic, and innovative projects. This is not to say that we should not dive deeply into any one literacy—quite the contrary. Each merits attention and, to demonstrate sophistication and increasing mastery, requires specific proficiency and knowledge. Residing within each of the literacies are also formative assessments and projects. For example, students could cultivate their ability to access and select digital applications, generate original video media productions, or investigate global issues pertaining to specific people and places. However, it is the point of intersection—the DMG project—that brings the literacies together into a genuine and engaging learning experience.

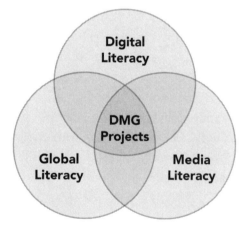

Figure 1.1: Intersection of DMG projects.

Basic Curriculum Design

Elegant curriculum design involves making deliberate choices. Every time we map out a unit of study or shape a lesson plan, we wrestle with the strategic selection of content, skills, assessment, and essential questions. The element of content is, I believe, the most demanding and formidable, in part because it involves the basic question of what we will leave out and what we will keep in terms of focus, timeliness, and power. But along the continuum of integration, we can deliver content to learners both within and across disciplines (Jacobs, 1989). At any point along that continuum, an intersection of the three new literacies has the potential to empower and propel the learner. The upgrading of skills occurs naturally, given that the new literacies entail inherently modern skills and strategies. For example, we may replace a traditional oral report with a videocast or poster that includes webpage design. Basic curriculum elements will remain evident in curriculum maps, but with the new literacies, teachers can move to a dynamic new outcome, a DMG project in which the new literacies meet. Projects are formative assessments that teachers have deliberately designed to provide evidence of this intersection.

DMG Projects in Action

When teachers are supported by principals to innovate their curriculum plans, the results immediately translate into corresponding learner engagement. The following section contains examples of schools that have deliberately integrated digital tools, media production, and global connections.

Sigsbee Charter School

Protecting life under the sea, a global issue, has been and continues to be the focus of a set of projects developed at the Sigsbee Charter School in Key West, Florida. All grade levels, K–8, are engaged in an interdisciplinary unit of study under the leadership of principal Elisa Jannes. Each grade-level teaching team selects an organizing topic for a focus, uses digital tools for investigation, and creates a presentation supported by media. For example, first-grade students used their knowledge of symbiotic relationships in marine environments to build little bird-tale books online (http://littlebirdtales.com). While completing the tales, students became illustrators, authors, and speakers.

The second-grade classes studied the health of the coral reef sea and created podcasts using Garage Band (www.garageband.com), posting them on their class websites to spread the word about protecting coral. The third-grade classes studied the classification of life through the lens of the local mangrove habitats.

Students developed multimedia presentations to disperse their knowledge of mangroves and featured them on student-created webpages using Yola (www.yola .com). In the future, the school is going to connect point to point with schools in Queensland, Australia, who are similarly focused on issues pertaining to the Great Barrier Reef and mangrove ecosystem preservation. Elisa notes that the work is long term and includes fieldwork, while incorporating the new literacies:

> Our middle school students are engaged in a multiyear authentic study of the coral reef in conjunction with Reef Relief and the rangers at the Dry Tortugas National Park, an island seventy miles west of Key West. They work with scientists in the classroom, travel to local beaches to collect data using some great equipment (including iPads and GoPros for presentations), and then do a comparison to the ecosystem out at the Dry Tortugas. Last year, a musically inclined group wrote a song with a local artist so that they could educate a broader community. You can hear the MP3 on our homepage. There is an accompanying video that students created for the grant report, and we are working on synthesizing the video clips and student-derived data from the Tortugas into one venue. Also, our fifth graders are camping in the Everglades this winter—a good opportunity for us to do similar work. (Personal communication, September 4, 2013).

It is clear that the choices made by the Sigsbee staff are rigorous, timely, and contemporary in their use of digital, media, and global connections.

Student News Action Network

A striking example of using media, digital tools, and global connectivity on the high school level is the Student News Action Network website (http://newsaction .org/). The service is hosted by the Washington International School (WIS), in Washington, DC, in partnership with the following regional bureau schools:

- **Africa**—American International School of Johannesburg
- **Asia and the Pacific**—Jakarta International School
- **Central and South Asia**—American School of Bombay
- **Europe**—American School of Paris
- **Middle East**—American School of Doha
- **South America**—Colegio Franklin Delano Roosevelt in Lima

The news action network has students participating from over fifty countries, posting articles and opinions, sharing media, and employing digital applications to survey responses. The website has a link to a wiki (http://wiki.newsaction .org) that provides coaching, with video clips by leading global journalists. This dynamic project is destined to motivate and empower students with new forms of communicating while integrating the great traditions of print journalism.

These examples reflect a deliberate decision to expand curriculum horizons and student learning opportunities by intersecting digital tools, media production, and global study.

Over the years I have sat reviewing curriculum maps, units, and lesson plans with teachers who have similarly taken the mundane and upgraded to a more engaging learning experience. Key to planning upgraded curriculum are choices regarding assessments.

Projects and Assessments as Reflections of What We Value

A starting or ending point in the curriculum-design process is the creation of meaningful student work. Assessment choices are like tribal totems, since they reveal what the local community and the society at large value. If we use multiple-choice exams taken with a no. 2 pencil, then we value the ability of a student to read a prompt, figure out the task, and choose the correct answer out of a limited set of possibilities. But what if were to use a modern fusion assessment that elevates connection globally, employs modern digital tools, supports media creation, and builds on classical print literacy?

The tools we use to inform our subject courses and unit preparation have a direct impact on content. The information from a paper textbook used to inform a study of contemporary content is dated once in print. And if the only evidence of learning my students generate is paper-based, they are limited in what they can demonstrate. If the four walls of the classroom limit perspective, then the world is left out. Use of the new literacies is not a sidebar, or worse, an *enrichment*. It is the necessary foundation for a 21st century learner.

Leader Actions

The intersection of digital, media, and global literacies is not only for curriculum and instructional design and communication enhancement. By openly modeling the use of the three literacies in administrative and professional tasks, leaders can create a culture conducive to growth. However, modeling alone is not sufficient. To formally introduce an upgrade in school communication, formal inquiry is necessary. A learning community is a natural focus group for conducting such a formal inquiry. As Andy Hargreaves and Michael Fullan (2012) discuss in *Professional Capital: Transforming Teaching in Every School*:

> Learning communities should be neither inconsequential talking shops nor a statistical world of scores and spreadsheets that take on a life of their own, far removed from real students. PLCs [professional learning communities] should be places where focused conversations and inquiries, supported by data and experience, lead to improvements and interventions that benefit real students whom the community shares in common. (p. 163)

Establishing the Rationale

In order to avoid the inconsequential and superficial trend-of-the-week initiative, leaders need solid pedagogical reasons for making changes and adjustments to a program. To provide a context and rationale for making key choices using digital, media, and global tools, I will reference my colleague Stephen Wilmarth (2010), who wrote an incisive chapter for *Curriculum 21: Essential Education for a Changing World* titled "Five Socio-Technology Trends That Change Everything in Learning and Teaching." I have added definitions to Wilmarth's five trends, as follows.

1. **Social production:** The democratization of knowledge creation, such as Wikipedia

2. **Social networks:** The building of communities from both random and focused groups worldwide, such as Facebook and Classroom 2.0

3. **Media grids:** The expanding media options available for students to demonstrate their learning

4. **Semantic web:** The programming of search engines to look by word frequency rather than logic, which can create some complications for learners

5. **Nonlinear learning:** When using a search engine, the fascinating but unrelated material we encounter that can lead to further searches

These five trends provide a rationale for faculties to revise classroom curriculum and instruction in order to incorporate DGM project-based learning. Certainly, in those schools that have organized themselves as PLCs, studying the potential application of the three literacies will be part of curriculum-planning workshops. As a starting point, a faculty makes a pledge to commit to integrating the literacies in at least one unit of one course per semester. At workshops, teacher groups pull up their units of study online and revise them by replacing a dated practice with one that reflects the new literacies. Sketches for DMG projects emerge while planning and brainstorming through the upgrading process.

I find it relatively easy to engage teachers in these types of upgrades, but what about the school administrator, curriculum chairperson, principal, school head, superintendent, or state education department official?

Upgrading Leadership

I propose that leaders begin by upgrading their own tasks, projects, and practices to incorporate digital, media, and global literacies. Leaders applying these five trends in a school aspiring to become a 21st century learning environment can find the process revitalizing. To begin, they list common and ongoing communication tasks with parents, teachers, students, or larger community entities. For each task, leaders identify the actual product (for example, memo, email announcement, flipchart, or agenda sheet) or event (faculty meeting, back-to-school night, or assembly) that is the occasion for the communication. Then they make a deliberate attempt to replace one of these traditional approaches with one or a combination of the three literacies. Finally, leaders monitor the effect the communication had on the intended audience.

Leading the Transit Scenarios

To demonstrate what upgraded leadership looks like, I encourage all school leaders (principals, district leaders, diocesans, department chairs, teacher leaders, and even state policy leaders) to create specific scenarios based on the common tasks a working group identifies. As we did with curriculum units, here we generate new angles and procedures for using the three literacies to improve the quality of the leadership process or task.

In the following sections, a series of specific scenarios using typical administrative tasks and responsibilities—faculty meetings, back-to-school night, the first day back to school for teachers, memos and announcements, and professional development days—demonstrate what such an exercise might look like. You and your leadership team can certainly generate your own set. The key is to think creatively, raise issues, and make the change.

Scenario One: Down With the Faculty Meeting

It is after school at Parker High. The empty hallways still hold the energy of the students who had been in motion through the school day. Clusters of teachers amble down the hall to the media center for their weekly faculty meeting.

Today they will not search for the seat furthest from the front or endure a litany of announcements from the assistant principal. Today will be different.

When the teachers enter the media center, there are laptops on the table adjacent to each chair. The principal, Stephen Nicholas, looks excited. The SMART Board has a PowerPoint slide that reads "Go to www.todaysmeet.com and join our backchannel." The teachers log in and find themselves in a closed chat room with the other teachers and see that Stephen has already posted a question. "Please share your most recent and effective web 2.0 application with your colleagues." The teachers respond:

- "I use www.visualthesaurus.com to help my kids with vocabulary."
- "I make statistics come alive with www.wolframalpha.com."
- "Try www.worldmapper.org to get your students to see visual representations of global demographics."

Without a word of preamble, the first fifteen minutes of the faculty meeting, before the face-to-face part of the meeting begins, are an active and engaged learning session in which everyone is energized and gets a few new ideas for classroom application as well. Stephen blogs every week about a local initiative or issue of concern and posts the agenda for these meetings on the school wiki.

Scenario Two: The Back-to-School Night Post-Webinar

In the past, Back to School Night was poorly attended because so many parents worked or could not set the night aside. Now it's different. Leonora Hale sets up a parent webinar series allowing her elementary students' parents to connect with other parents and interact with faculty members and department heads. The parents and students enjoy the convenience of being able to access the archive of any of the past webinar programs. Face-to-face meetings are actually more effective and engaging, because she has already exchanged much of the standardized information. The best part of this scenario is that Leonora's fifth graders run the webinar platform.

Scenario Three: Interactive Website Versus the Paper Chase

It is 3:00 p.m., and the bell is ringing relentlessly. The buses are here. Fifth-grade teacher Sylvia James has had to raise her voice so her kids can hear her final instructions. "Be sure you have the field trip papers for your parents. Neatly fold them and put them in your backpack. Your parents need to sign them. Bring them back tomorrow, or you don't get to go to the nature center. Also, remember the other paper about the test schedule. Don't forget your math homework. Have a good night. Goodbye."

Now, if Sylvia taught in Leonora's school, she would have more effective communication options. Leonora has worked with the information technology (IT) department and her staff to create a vibrant and dynamic interactive school website that is both attractive and easy to navigate. One page contains memos, announcements, and forms that parents can download and return via email. Another has videos of the students' most recent performances (including the third-grade recorder concert) for parents to proudly view. Leonora also writes a monthly blog post for both students and parents on current issues and decisions facing the school. The school's website is a virtual town square filled with photos, life, and activity.

Scenario Four: The Flipped Superintendent's Conference Day

It is the end of August, and teachers in Cherry Valley School District are having their ritual first day back to school. Everyone mills around in front of the auditorium drinking coffee and eating donuts. Faculty and staff reconnect and then crowd into the auditorium. Prime seats for this event are along the back row. The superintendent welcomes everyone back, provides an update on the state of school initiatives, and introduces the fourteen new hires, who dutifully stand up, smile, and sit down, and then everyone settles in for the keynote speaker. Most faculty members don't even need to be present to know exactly how the meeting ends.

A neighboring district plans things differently. Amy Mendoza, the school superintendent, knows that more than anything her teaching faculty wants to get to school and get started. She does not need to involve them in the startup agenda. She decides to flip the conference day's agenda and uses digital and media tools to do so. Rather than asking teachers to show up early in the morning, she has created a short with a wonderfully clear message about the upcoming year. She has also included video interviews with the newly hired teachers so that the rest of the faculty can learn something about each of them. Amy sends the video out two weeks before the first day of school, along with a link to Socrative (www.socrative .com). On that site, she includes resources and links describing the most important initiatives for her staff to review, with a response component. Three keynote speeches will be live streamed throughout the district, recorded, and archived. The social event occurs at the end of the day, with ample donuts and coffee.

Scenario Five: Opening the Professional Development Window With Intercontinental Colleagues

Ryan Roberts, a seasoned middle school principal in the Pacific Northwest, knows that professional development at the end of a long school day spent with thirteen-year-olds is tough on teachers. As he puts it, "My teachers are not feeling so perky" at that time. Ryan cares about his staff and is concerned about the idea of linking professional development credits with attendance. It feels like the old *seat time* imposed on the students. His idea is to upgrade and open global portals as the school considers its mathematics program and its alignment with the Common Core State Standards (CCSS). Going through the Classroom 2.0 website, he locates two schools using different approaches to mathematics for his staff to interact with; one is in upstate New York, and the other in Singapore. Using Skype, he records the point-to-point sessions. The three schools establish a workgroup on Edmodo (www.edmodo.com) for sharing and interaction using a time frame that accommodates even the twelve-hour time difference, and the staff is enlivened.

Sharing scenarios about upgrading leadership practice is of great value, since much of the learning is new and untried. The key is to focus on deliberate application of digital, media, and global literacy and to develop new solutions collaboratively.

Conclusion

With the emergence of the new literacies, we are seeing inevitable and exciting iterations of teaching and learning. It follows, then, that notions about leading our schools and education communities are shifting fundamentally. Traditional hierarchical forms of leadership are giving way to virtual task management and more collaborative planning. This shift is evident in day-to-day operations. The focus is less about making a schedule for a meeting in a specific room in a school setting and more about the way we are dealing with immediate communication.

In examining the intersections of digital, media, and global literacies in curriculum planning, we find that there are implications for leadership, for in order to support the contemporary learner, we must ourselves be digitally literate, media savvy, and globally connected education leaders.

References and Resources

Apkon, S. (2013). *The age of the image: Redefining literacy in a world of screens.* New York: Farrar, Straus and Giroux.

Gee, J. P., & Hayes, E. R. (2011). *Language and learning in the digital age.* New York: Routledge.

Hargreaves, A., & Fullan, M. (2012). *Professional capital: Transforming teaching in every school.* New York: Teachers College Press.

Jacobs, H. H. (Ed.). (1989). *Interdisciplinary curriculum: Design and implementation.* Alexandria, VA: Association for Supervision and Curriculum Development.

Jacobs, H. H. (Ed.). (2010). *Curriculum 21: Essential education for a changing world.* Alexandria, VA: Association for Supervision and Curriculum Development.

Mansilla, V. B., & Jackson, A. (2011). *Educating for global competence: Preparing our youth to engage the world.* New York: Asia Society.

National Governors Association Center for Best Practices & Council of Chief State School Officers. (2010). *Common Core State Standards for English language arts and literacy in history/social science, science, & technical subjects.* Washington, DC: Authors. Accessed at www.corestandards.org/assets/CCSSI_ELA%20Standards .pdf on September 9, 2013.

Than, K. (2012, June 14). *World's oldest cave art found—made by Neanderthals?* Accessed at http://news.nationalgeographic.com/news/2012/06/120614 -neanderthal-cave-paintings-spain-science-pike on April 12, 2013.

Wilmarth, S. (2010). Five socio-technological trends that are changing everything in teaching and learning. In H. H. Jacobs (Ed.), *Curriculum 21: Essential education for a changing world* (pp. 80–96). Alexandria, VA: Association for Supervision and Curriculum Development.

Jeanne Tribuzzi, EdM, is the assistant superintendent for curriculum, instruction, and professional development at Global Concepts Charter School in Lackawanna, New York. She has been an educator for twenty-four years.

Jeanne has served in a variety of roles—as a primary classroom teacher, multiage teacher, middle school English teacher, director of staff development, and director of English language arts, English as a second language, and second languages. She is pursuing her doctorate at the University of Buffalo in educational leadership and policy.

A Curriculum 21 faculty member, Jeanne has also worked with U.S. and international schools to map and align curriculum and implement best-practice literacy instruction. She lives in Orchard Park, New York, with her family.

To learn more about Jeanne's work, follow her on Twitter @jtribuzzi.

Michael L. Fisher, EdM, is an educational consultant and instructional coach working with schools and districts in the United States and Canada to sustain curriculum-mapping initiatives and implement instructional technology. He specializes in the integration of research-based instructional strategies to facilitate transformations of curriculum design, instructional practice, and professional collaboration around 21st century fluencies, Common Core State Standards, and digital tools.

In addition to his graduate degree in English education, Michael has post baccalaureate certificates in teaching science, English language arts, and gifted education. He has taught a variety of grade levels and content areas over the years, primarily in middle schools. He is an active blogger on his own as well as on Curriculum 21's blog and on ASCD's social network EDge (http://edge.ascd.org). Michael is the author of *Upgrade Your Curriculum: Practical Ways to Transform Units and Engage Students*.

To learn more about Michael's work, visit his website, The Digigogy Collaborative (www.digigogy.com), or follow him on Twitter @fisher1000.

To book Jeanne Tribuzzi or Michael L. Fisher for professional development, contact pd@solution-tree.com.

Chapter 2
Bridging Traditional and Modern Literacy

By Jeanne Tribuzzi and Michael L. Fisher

Teachers and school leaders face a meteor shower of choices every day, and the fast pace that defines the culture of 21st century schools leaves them little time for study and collaboration. Yet these school and community leaders, tasked with creating a vision for modernizing work beyond simply putting computers in classrooms, must collaborate and plan strategically in order to upgrade the way our students connect and communicate. At the same time, they must balance modernization with traditions worth keeping.

In reality, it takes an interconnected global village to tackle the challenges to schools' current practices around new literacies. It is the goal of this chapter to share a variety of ideas and models that schools can use to meet those challenges. To that end, we will explore the various facets of the new literacy and introduce the modern literacy continuum. In a series of examples entitled "Continuum Coach," we will examine the bridge from the traditional to the modern and explore traditional practices through modern lenses.

How are you interacting with this text? Traditional book? E-reader? Online book preview? Audiobook? Quote on Twitter? Discussion in a chat room? Once scarce, information is now explosive in both amount and variety of formats. The fact that there are so many different ways to access this text is a reflection of the changed literacy environment. How we acquire information and what we do with it is as much a function of the form of communication as it is of social constructs around comprehension and the remixing and sharing of ideas. We have an obligation to continue to build the traditional foundations of literacy, but we must simultaneously develop literacy in other areas: technological literacy; information literacy; media, global, and social literacy; and more. In short, we must build a brand new version of modern literacy.

CONTINUUM COACH: THE MIDDLE SCHOOL SUMMER READING PROJECT

In the summer of 2011, a mutual friend's daughter who was entering the tenth grade was explaining her summer English language arts project to us. The book she and her classmates were to read and explore was Orson Scott Card's *Ender's Game*. We were so excited to hear about the book choice, as it opened up myriad discussions of and connections to topics like bullying, popular music, the future, other books such as *The Hunger Games*, text elements like point of view and style, worldwide political events, foreign policy, and so on.

We asked her how much she had already read, and she responded, "I haven't started yet." Our level of excitement and her level of excitement were in two completely different orbits. She explained that it was like all of the other book projects she'd ever done, and she was bored—before she ever started reading. Why?

The project, per her teacher's parameters, involved reading the book, answering comprehension questions, defining thirty in-text words, finding ten important quotes, and writing a one-page paper summarizing the text using at least three of the quotes.

We noticed that our friend's daughter had an iPad among the stack of books and papers she was carrying. Nodding toward the iPad, we told her that her project was kind of halfway done. She lit up and asked us to tell her what we meant. We downloaded *Ender's Game* to the device through the Kindle app and asked her to open the book. We showed her how to search in the text for keywords in the teacher's comprehension questions so she could easily find the answers. We showed her how to click on words and get definitions and searchable resources. We also shared with her how to access popular quotes in the book that a global audience of readers had already identified. Additionally, we introduced her to the website Shmoop and pointed out all of the resources for developing a one-page paper. Finally, we showed her how to give attribution for the information she found and used, emphasizing that the work needed to be hers, not just a copy-and-paste job.

She was thrilled that her task had been made shorter and easier, but she wasn't completely sold on using the device to "skirt the system." She told us it seemed like cheating. We reminded her that she still had to read the book and that her work with it needed to be thoughtful. We told her that technology allows us to do things better than we have in the past, not to mention faster.

What we wanted to explain was that a decades-old comfort zone should not impede learning. We wanted to tell this teenager that it was really her teacher who was cheating, passing off preparation for the 1950s as college and career readiness. But we did not.

This anecdote was transformational for us on two levels: (1) students, not just their teachers, see modern learning methods as cheating, and (2) this is the next moment in the evolution of literacy.

We did tell her that what we explored on her digital device was the *beginning* of the learning process, not the intended product. We explained that the engagement in the learning was through the exploration of a new way to access and process information. The intended learning was still going to happen, albeit in a different way than what the teacher had planned. We told her that her teacher would probably also see what we did as cheating and that it might be a good idea to share with her teacher what she discovered and her excitement about it, explaining that she had simply discovered new and exciting ways to do what was required. Perhaps that would spark a change to the teacher's project. (Note that we didn't refer to this as the "student's project.")

This student's assignment falls under the category of product-driven instruction. All that matters in this instructional activity is what is done, not what is learned. Everything, including the learning, is variable, except for the product.

Modern learning practice demands a deeper authenticity to instruction than the traditional model of literacy in schools—in this case, reading a book in isolation over the summer and writing a summary about it.

There are so many opportunities to bridge the modern literacy continuum. Besides access to digital devices and web tools, it has become the norm for students to access information in a variety of formats, including textual, visual, interactive digital, and audio. Additionally, there are opportunities for comparative analysis between services like Shmoop, CliffsNotes, and SparkNotes. What kinds of conversations, presentations, and collaborative products could students create when considering access to multiple types of media around the summer reading project?

It is not okay for some classrooms to embrace such an approach and some to sit it out; when it comes to teachers, families should not have to depend on the luck of the draw. Including new literacies can't depend on whether the teacher is comfortable in this new arena; it has to be the expectation for everyone in the school. Small gaps in instruction early on will lead to canyon-sized gaps as students get older.

The more teachers study and work together to ensure that curriculum design and instructional practice always include web tools, apps, programs, and devices, the more pointed and appropriate the use of new tools will be. At the same time, we must keep in mind that we don't use the tool for its own sake but to accomplish the literacy work at hand. This work will grow in complexity and depth as students' ability to practice, problem solve, collaborate virtually, compose, and become fluent with the new literacies increases. Each grade level will build on the work of the previous one, and the genres students work in will expand to include blogging, tweeting, writing online reviews, collaborating in Google Drive (formerly Google Docs), and much more. Choosing the right tools to support student work is part of the process of deliberate curriculum design and instructional practice.

Aspects of Modern Literacy

Modern literacy is about the evolution from traditional reading, writing, listening, and speaking to using multiple types of print and digital media, online communication, and collaborative structures to enable depth in learning and knowledge for the sake of sharing ideas and communicating in a global society. With modern literacy, students receive and express communication beyond the narrow use of traditional print.

Access

Like the printing press following its invention in the fifteenth century, the Internet and other forms of electronic communication have exponentially expanded access to information. Schools need to be working with a sense of urgency to upgrade curriculum to include these new technologies and literacies.

At the same time, classical print literacy is alive and well in our classrooms, and research on reading achievement supports the practice of keeping our classrooms teeming with quality literature and nonfiction texts in order to engage students in the reading process (Allington, 2009). Providing classrooms with high-quality libraries for independent reading and giving students time to read in school result in better readers (Krashen, 2004). To eventually read well, students must also read voluminously (Allington, 1977). Whether they are reading text in hard copy, on tablets, or on other reading devices, access to a plethora of rich reading resources is of the highest importance. Mobile devices have become the new normal for adolescents; it is how they prefer to access as well as communicate text. However, it may be some time before schools have expanded their resources enough to equip every student with a laptop or mobile device to use for the entire day. Whether students read on a screen or in a print book, comprehension is still the brass ring, and both venues require stamina, strong reading skills, and critical thinking.

Communication and Engagement

The purpose of any literacy program is ultimately the meaningful communication of ideas, not simply the mastery of a set of isolated skills. Unfortunately, it is the latter that sometimes makes up the bulk of low-quality literacy programs for students. The Common Core State Standards have given us clear expectations that all students will reach new, rigorous levels of reading in all classrooms. The anchor standards for reading expect students to read with a critical eye, analyze an author's language, and identify his or her point of view (NGA & CCSSO, 2010).

Learning to read and write are complex human processes. Each has both cognitive and communicative properties. We read to make meaning and understand, and we write to communicate with others while working through a process of clarifying and organizing our thoughts. Critical to growth in reading and writing is engagement, with comprehension and expression as the consistent goals (Guthrie, Wigfield, & You, 2012). Students should be engaged in the writing process through explicit instruction in the quality traits of writing and a variety of genres, both traditional and new. Modern literacy is evolutionary—rooted in the traditional and considerate of multiple types and interactions of media. According to Lucy Calkins, Mary Ehrenworth, and Christopher Lehman (2012) in *Pathways to the Common Core*, the following principles are important to accelerating the reading achievement of students.

> Students should be doing lots and lots of in-school reading. In elementary schools, there has been a lot of research about dedicating time to independent reading, to moving kids as rapidly as possible up levels of text, and to teaching higher-level reading skills within

the books they are each reading. Thousands of schools have done that work and shown tremendous reading progress. (p. 69)

Teachers can teach the early literacy skills of concepts of print, such as letter and word recognition, directionality, phonemic awareness, and phonics, not only with authentic literature and explicit instruction but with hundreds of apps that are widely available for tablets and mobile devices. The growing availability of apps for teaching early literacy skills has the potential to differentiate instruction more granularly and to engage students with games and activities that embed practice with these foundational concepts and skills. Piloting and evaluating those tools must become the new normal for primary classrooms. Authentic reading and writing for meaning are still the end goals, but intervention and practice with components of language can add a new level of support and engagement for students.

Teachers are obligated to leverage these new tools to increase and expand the amount of time students are engaged in modern literacy work throughout the school day and beyond, and this must occur in a well-planned, deliberate way. Process is essential as schools begin the journey of modernizing students' literacy work.

Navigation and Filtering

In the googling culture we have created, students can find information, resources, and media, but they are not necessarily able to evaluate their worth or accuracy or articulate their relevance. While access to information has never been easier, navigation and filtering of information has never been more difficult. In order to be literate in the 21st century, students must know how to filter the vast amounts of information they discover. In the new world of modern literacy, the modern teacher's responsibility lies in ensuring that students access its depths as well as its breadth.

There is often an assumption that students are knowledgeable about navigating the Internet and other technologies—that they can locate and gather information quickly. This assumption may be true for Facebook, Google, and other sites teens tend to frequent, but it may not be true beyond social media. Teachers we've worked with over the years frequently tell us that students tend to take the first three or four results of a Google search as their sources when doing research. These students are more likely to copy and paste what they find online without attribution than they are to filter and connect the ideas and create something new (Fisher, 2012a).

Despite the lack of explicit instruction, from the time of adolescence students begin a journey toward proficiency with social media. In fact, most people can become fluent in the use of casual social media without too much work. The engagement factor is high, while the prerequisite skills needed to succeed are fairly low. However, educators should not assume that shifting students' online navigational skills to scholarly or complex areas will happen as easily.

Teaching students how to locate vetted, reliable information, perhaps through national or educational databases, requires that we explicitly incorporate online navigation and filtering into our curricula in specific and progressively sophisticated ways. Expecting that the library media specialist will cover it is not sufficient. Higher-level application must happen in all classrooms throughout a student's school career if we are to expect a shift in practice.

Schools need to develop K–12 vertically aligned plans for scaffolding what a student should be able to do from one grade level to the next with regard to discovering useful and relevant information and evaluating it for accuracy and reliability. Teachers must use media and information tools systematically across grade levels, and expectations about employing them must become part of the curriculum.

To express their own claims or arguments and to support their view with evidence from valid sources, students can use a variety of platforms and formats. They can present what they know and have learned in so many ways that extend beyond paper. Visuals, audio, and multimedia, including Internet tools and apps, are those modern extensions.

The Continuum of Modern Literacy

Rather than emphasizing a single media, modern literacy uses a variety of tools and technologies, from traditional to modern. Figure 2.1 (page 32) reframes literacy as a collection of interconnections along a continuum. Students and teachers can enter this continuum at any point, depending on the goals of the work to be done.

Thus, creating a modern literacy program is not so much about following a sequence of steps as it is about knowing where one is situated on the continuum at a given instructional moment. No matter where you enter, however, modern literacy instruction asks that one consider the other elements of the continuum.

On the consumer side, the focus is on traditional print and common ways of accessing multimedia. This could mean alternative types of media or integrated media such as magazine articles that have pictures, diagrams, or visual data. The audience is primarily reading, viewing, or interpreting the media for the sake of

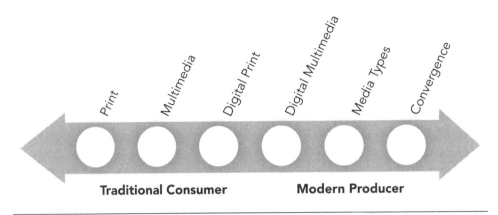

Figure 2.1: The continuum of modern literacy.

comprehension and knowledge but not necessarily to begin research, create a new product, or remix the information for a different level of cognition or presentation.

In the middle of the continuum, the digital print and multimedia are mainly digital versions of traditional formats. Part of the evolution at this point is developing an ability to interact easily with all types of media, including social media; to remix them into a different presentation; and—as is the case with links embedded in a digital text—to access additional, related media within the primary source.

On social networking sites like Twitter and Facebook, media consumers share and filter information. These digital media allow users to easily grab and connect pieces of media from different sources to allow further connections and synthesis beyond the intent of a single source. Media consumers can access digital media through websites and web-enabled devices, such as a Kindle, where every word or image is hyperlinked to additional information. Social interactions and hyperlinks are the bridge to the producer end of the continuum. On the producer side, students create traditional print and digital media, images, audio, video, presentations, infographics, charts, data visualizations, maps, and diagrams and integrate any or all of these.

Educators should be looking to enhance and evolve their programs and make them more sophisticated, because the ultimate goal of modern literacy instruction is the *convergence zone*. This is where we leverage multiple types of literacy, media, and devices for maximum learning. The impetus is to teach students to engage with multiple types of media for constructing meaning while also focusing on priority pieces.

Students need opportunities to be literate and then transfer that literacy into unconscious ease of use, or *fluency*; they should be able to think within and problem solve through their learning while considering and engaging multiple forms along the continuum. Getting this to work in reality takes strong leadership, a vision for the work, and buy-in from all stakeholders, including students. It also means making the technology, tools, and resources an immersive part of *all* instruction rather than features of a planned-for event, such as computer-lab Thursdays or devices on rotating carts that classes see only once every two weeks.

Media and Literacy Convergence

In *Convergence Culture*, Henry Jenkins (2008) writes:

> Convergence requires media companies to rethink old assumptions about what it means to consume media, assumptions that shape both programming and marketing decisions. If old consumers were assumed to be passive, the new consumers are active. If old consumers were predictable and stayed where you told them to stay, then new consumers are migratory, showing a declining loyalty to networks or media. If old consumers were isolated individuals, the new consumers are more socially connected. If the work of media consumers was once silent and invisible, the new consumers are now noisy and public. (p. 12)

While this comment refers to business and marketing, we think it also applies to education, specifically media, digital, and global literacy. The dichotomy here, however, is not between media companies and consumers but between teachers and students. Teachers who might be in a complacent zone are at odds with students who were born into social public noise. Where literacy used to entail reading and writing, it has now become a launching pad from which the other literacies take off. Literacy has exploded in terms of meaning, learning, and mechanism. The forms and functions of literacy are as intricately connected as a spider web. At this point in the 21st century, the design for literacy instruction is for interconnectedness at a level far above anything we have ever imagined, and the modern purpose becomes to connect—and then make new connections.

We need basic literacies, but we also need what is beyond them—those literacies that demand presentation, problem solving, relevance, truthfulness of resources, and collaborative construction. Modern literacy is multifaceted, multimodal, and multigenre. It is globally considerate and properly attributed. It is socially constructed, thought provoking, and interactive. It is big, loud, and conspicuous, rooted in strong content knowledge and created for sharing with multiple audiences and purposes.

Some teachers read this as a path to their own irrelevance or as a challenge to "the way we've always done it." It is quite the opposite. There has never before been a time when a teacher is more needed than right now. Students need guides as they navigate the new world. They need coaches to direct them in solving authentic problems. They need teachers who are just as plugged in as they are and literate on multiple levels.

There is a humorous video floating around the Internet that features a student trying to read a traditional print textbook in a classroom. He pokes at pictures, tries to click on words, and exclaims, "This is a foreign tool" (Lehmann, 2009). While the video is a metaphorical jab at the value placed on the traditional print texts, it illustrates the fact that our digital natives have an expectation of the media they consume: it has to be interactive.

For centuries, *literacy* meant simply competence with the written language, extended to new learning from reading, explorations through writing, and critical thinking through rich discussion. First we learned to read, and then we read to learn. In the 21st century, literacy has a much broader meaning, and the implications are infinite. What we are looking for is a new, modern version of *fluency*, which is well beyond just literate. In an article for *SmartBlog on Education*, Fisher (2012a) writes:

> Students need to be able to do what the sixth capacity of the College and Career Readiness Capacities is asking of students: Students use technology and digital media strategically and capably. "Strategic and capable" means that digital literacy is about more than exposure, knowledge, and adequate levels of competence. It means that students need choices, toolboxes and opportunities to evaluate relevant resources. This is what I call "solution fluency." Students need to go well beyond digital and technological literacy to be fluent in our modern learning landscapes.

Solution fluency is about access and navigation—knowing what resources are potentially available, how to access those resources, and how to determine their usefulness and relevance. Solution fluency is about solving a problem using the toolboxes and resources a student has collected over the course of his or her academic career. All of the literacies, including digital, media, and global literacy, are only as good as the ways in which they are navigated and in how connected they might be in terms of the continuum. In order for them to be effective strategies for college and career readiness, these literacies must be experienced as ubiquitous and interconnected elements in a student's academic experience. Thus, solution fluency is about how students find the resources they need, and the learning becomes about how the interconnections—the convergences—inform and enrich the content pieces.

We needed to have support for digital, media, and global literacy in place *yesterday*, or we are choosing to leave kids behind, satisfied with preparing them for a decade that has already passed. We once exalted teachers for planning Thursday's computer lab, believing that those teachers were preparing students for the new world. That's no longer enough.

Future Forward: Transmedia

We live in a time of creative and disruptive moments. Each of those moments could easily overtake another, or they can blend and produce something exciting, fresh, and brand new. This latter view of literacy instruction is sometimes referred to as *transmedia*. While much of what is usually defined as transmedia relates to storytelling, the definition is really more encompassing, allowing for a text infused with images, film, animations, and sounds, all adding up to a multimodal version of literacy heretofore unseen. We would like to suggest that transmedia is the new wave of literacy instruction, based on the blending and remixing of all facets of literacy, text, and media types. In his book *I Live in the Future & Here's How It Works*, Nick Bilton (2010) writes:

> Just like me, the generation coming of age in this digital society doesn't see or perceive much difference in types of media. Video? Words? Music? Computer code? It doesn't matter. The actual tools being used are irrelevant. It's the end result—the storylines, the messages—that matters. This generation thinks in pictures, words, still and moving images, and is comfortable mixing them all in the same space. (p. 12)

Transmedia is not a new term, but digital tools have expanded its meaning by making it easier to engage multiple modalities. All of this lends itself to a more participatory learning event; what used to be an individual linear act of reading and responding is now a collaborative construct with multiple viewpoints and opportunities for enhancement and revision.

On the popular social media blog *Mashable*, contributor Lisa Hsia (2011) writes:

> Technology has created tools that allow the user to interact and gamify content as never before (location-based, virtual goods, augmented reality, QR codes, etc). Fans' familiarity with and desire to experience TV content across devices other than TV has exploded.

Hsia extols the popularity of transmedia in television, where the use of inter-activity and multiple platforms is not only becoming the norm but also a good economic decision in terms of how content is delivered. Many of you reading this are already aware of this shift. When was the last time you watched something on television and either tweeted, wrote a Facebook post, purchased a product, or watched additional media related to it? Given the breadth of available opportunities, even the most die-hard Luddites among us are hard-pressed not to be participants in the interactivity of new literacies.

Digital tools make transmedia a new form and position us on the cusp of an avalanche of interactive and social learning opportunities. We have an obligation to teach our students to function in this world now, or they will become viewers outside the bubble of participation, effectively useless to future employers.

In order for convergence and transmedia to enable students to make meaning in multiple modern ways, educators need to integrate them into modern curriculum design and practice.

A New Model of Balanced Literacy

The premise of a balanced literacy program, depicted in figure 2.2 (page 37), is that students will experience teacher coaching and modeling and plenty of inde-pendent practice with reading, writing, listening, and speaking and will contin-ually receive feedback to move to the next level of sophistication, with varying levels of teacher support. Assessment in such a program must be comprehensive and include both content learning and process-based work. At the elementary level, formative assessment often needs to be individualized, so students can spend time acquiring new reading and writing skills while working at the appropriate difficulty level, either alone or with teacher guidance. Students should also spend abundant time working independently to apply their growing reading and writing skills to ensure growth in proficiency, as well as reading and writing in the service of content-area knowledge. Stamina and the ability to concentrate for extended periods of time are necessary skills that teachers must cultivate and expect in classroom work.

Moving to a new model of balanced literacy requires the inclusion of new opportunities for access and interaction, with the goal of attaining a new level of sophistication, new audiences, and interconnectedness. Strong reading and writ-ing will always be necessary, and the expanded opportunities for collaboration and interaction with authentic audiences—audiences beyond the teacher that are relevant to purpose or task—will raise the level of meaningful reading, writing, and communication. Reading expectations for students beyond grade 3 should also include close reading or deep textual analysis per the Common Core State

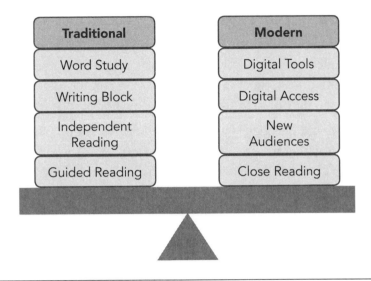

Figure 2.2: A new model of balanced literacy.

Standards (NGA & CCSSO, 2010). Teachers should introduce these skills once students are reading more sophisticated texts with support for analyzing and interpreting the structure and art of the written word.

Let's look at each element of this model in turn.

Word Study

Word study begins at the emergent literacy stages with concepts of print, alphabetic principles, spelling patterns, morphology, and vocabulary, and this work should move right through to the high school level with the study of etymology and explicit instruction in academic vocabulary. The expansion of tools that continues to support and engage students in word study will bring these concepts to life like never before. We must be clear on the outcomes of word study—accurate encoding and decoding of print, conventional spelling, and expansive vocabulary knowledge and usage. A growing number of resources exist for this work, yet having an expected progression in place and instruction that expects the transfer of these skills to reading, writing, speaking, and listening is critical. That is the end goal for all literacy work.

Writing Block

Blocks of time devoted to writing instruction must be part of each school day, and students must spend this time on authentic work involving the writing process. Students must be taught various writing genres and content-area writing.

Whether they are writing on a computer, on paper, on a mobile device, or with some other digital tool, the process of generating ideas, drafting, revising, and editing is fundamental to writing success. A curriculum should be established that ensures students progress up the ladder of sophistication and complexity in writing throughout their school career. For this to occur, for students to continue to grow as writers, they must write daily, both in school and at home.

Instruction should include (1) modeling and feedback from teachers who are well versed in teaching writing and using modern tools such as Google Drive to share work, (2) an online thesaurus to embellish vocabulary, and (3) various word-processing tools to track changes and provide feedback from teacher to student and student to student. Each grade should have explicit instructional expectations with regard to certain genre and completed "published" pieces aligned to rubrics to support assessment and portfolio expectations. For instance, students in first grade will receive instruction in narrative writing and produce several personal narratives by the end of the unit. They will also learn to write nonfiction books as well as persuasive book reviews and procedural writing of some type.

Three types of writing outlined in the Common Core standards (NGA & CCSSO, 2010), narrative, informational/explanatory, opinion/argument, must be included in each grade level K–12 via a variety of genre that fit under the umbrellas of those writing types. Teachers must also include new approaches to writing in formats such as blogs, email, Twitter feeds, Skype interviews, and online reviews within these genre expectations and progressions. Although publication takes many forms, the writing process and skills of writing remain fundamental to functioning in the new public and digital world.

Independent Reading

The CCSS make it very clear that one of the major goals of schools is to produce strong, independent critical readers (NGA & CCSSO, 2010). In order to meet this goal, students must spend time alone with texts engaged in the independent, cognitive work of reading. A block of time for independent reading should take place in K–12 classrooms each day, since not every student can be expected to practice at home. We must practice any human endeavor in which we hope to achieve or improve performance. Skill development, whether we're talking about sports or reading, is always in service of improved performance in the real game.

Classrooms should include the vast array of devices that humans now use to read. Students must become proficient readers in traditional reading venues, as well as with the modern devices that have become so prevalent. One is not more important than the other; all are grounded in the skills and cognitive strategies that take place in the mind of the reader. If we are to meet the goal of building strong readers who are capable of the analysis and interpretation of complex texts, we must ensure that along with some quiet time each day for focused concentration in the act of reading, students receive instruction in the strategies that good readers use. In curriculum that expects students to move along a progression from learning to read to reading to learn, some choice and ownership over what they read is also critical to student engagement. Because this level of individualized instruction allows for targeted assessment and feedback, teachers should be conferring with students as independent reading is happening in the classroom. They should not be taking care of other tasks while students go through the motions of reading silently. The instructional period must be beneficial to students and not extra time for teachers.

Guided Reading

According to Irene Fountas and Gay Su Pinnell (1996), "Guided reading is a context in which a teacher supports each reader's development of effective strategies for processing novel texts at increasingly challenging levels of difficulty" (p. 2). Typically, during guided reading, the teacher chooses texts that are at an appropriate level of difficulty to read with small groups, and the texts offer one or two new things for students to learn. The focus of the instruction is making meaning and teaching students various strategies to use when decoding or comprehending ideas or concepts they have not yet met in print. The students have support as they read with the teacher, and they will often read the text several times to gain independence and fluency. The end goal of guided reading is that students transfer the taught skills and strategies to their own independent reading. In many instances, students spend a good deal of time with guided reading but without the appropriate time for transfer and practice in independent reading. With all of the new venues for reading that exist in the digital world, teachers must expand guided reading to include websites, blogs, and other forms of digital print. The online world of reading is also increasingly available to younger and younger children, and our classroom instruction must adapt.

Before that transfer happens to fully independent reading, guided reading begins to morph into shared reading, where the pairs or small groups share the same piece of text in a variety of ways. Shared reading can happen with a big book, a set of class books, a displayed web page, a shared article that students will annotate, or a text that is shared on a computer or tablet. This type of reading often sees teachers taking students through text that is slightly out of reach for their full independent comprehension. As they read, students together learn both disciplinary and literary content and comprehension strategies. As students get older, this shared reading will become *close reading*. The sophistication of shared or close reading will become textual analysis and interpretation.

Digital Tools

Digital tools such as web 2.0 interactive websites, device-specific applications such as apps on an iPad or Droid device, even software that lives on a specific computer like Microsoft Word, Mac's Pages, or Inspiration are all part of the modern literacy landscape. These tools help students both consume and produce media for the sake of integration and convergence. Planning for the use of individual tools is not nearly as important as making sure students have a toolbox of resources to pull from during instruction. This means that using an interactive whiteboard or a digital presentation tool is secondary; students must know how to leverage the technology that will be useful. If they do not have a particular tool in their toolbox, it becomes a teacher's responsibility to help them discover and explore potential tools but not necessarily to teach isolated lessons about them. Students should have opportunities for both exploration and demonstration of the tools in their toolboxes, with coaching as necessary.

Digital Access

Information now lives everywhere. Students can access information and content from traditional and digital texts, online resources, virtual opportunities, and multimedia—but only if we grant them access. We limit learning when we limit access. Schools should be places of expansive learning rather than prisons of content. The level of access we are advocating opens up a complex issue, however, involving Internet filters that block access to sites that could potentially be useful for student learning, the infrastructure needed for Internet access, and the availability of digital devices.

Part of the problem is that many technology coordinators know more about infrastructure than they do about education, and part is due to wildly divergent interpretations of the Children's Internet Protection Act (CIPA). Students need to be protected, of course, but not mass blocked. Teachers should have the right to grant access in the classroom, and there should be procedures in place for students to submit their own websites for consideration. We cannot engage modern instruction without seriously reconsidering how we filter content and tools, particularly social tools, at school. While some would disagree, our world is shifting to a more social and interactive one, both physically and online, and students must be prepared to use the tools of the world they live in. If we don't teach appropriate usage and continue to limit access and if there is limited availability of devices, how will students know what to do when they graduate and move on to college or careers? Knowing the difference between right and wrong behavior around technology will evolve only when students have access and are explicitly taught how to use online tools.

Access gives our students the 21st century skills they need to be successful in the world: communication skills, collaboration skills, critical-thinking skills, and creative problem-solving skills. Access to all of the information available is extremely important in our modern literacy landscape. We teach students about relevancy, importance, and usefulness—all functions of filtering.

CONTINUUM COACH: UPGRADING THE MEDIA CENTER

The library media center in a typical school has been a key player in digital access. The first computers were usually housed there, and the media specialist helped to direct a building's literacy traffic from there.

In terms of the modern literacy continuum, the media center is still important, but it needs to expand its functions and location. In fact, the media center is no longer the media center—the school is, with every teacher now responsible for literacy in some way. Likewise, the media specialist's function is no longer about what lives in the library but about what types of media live everywhere in a student's accessible landscape of literacy opportunities throughout the school, community, and world. In the 21st century, the media specialist should take on an evolved role as the cornerstone of modern literacy in a school.

A November 2012 visit to a middle school media center in western New York State yielded a media specialist's treasure trove of literacy opportunities that all stakeholders contributed to: students, teachers, and even an administrator! Around the school, there were Quick Response (QR) codes that students could scan with their digital devices (the school had both iPads and Kindles for student use, as well as a policy that allowed smartphones); these codes gave them information related to what teachers were teaching at the time and provided opportunities for additional information in multiple media formats and for formative assessment.

Teachers, students, and the administrator all contributed content that students could scan and either read, listen to, or view (depending on whether the contributor created a written book report, an oral book report, or a video response that was housed

Continued →

online) before making a decision to check out a print book. The media specialist was working to add these digital creations to the search system as well as to make it easier to access the associated media. The media specialist told us that there was a high degree of excitement and engagement when students used their peers' and teachers' creations to make decisions about whether or not to check out a book. Students increased their level of participation and comprehension as they interacted with the books and the additional supporting information shared through the QR codes.

There are many opportunities here. Media specialists can begin to think of their role in moving schools beyond traditional print literacy; engaging teachers with elements of the continuum, specifically around text supports that evolve traditional media; and making other media available for learning—print, nonprint, visual, audio, digital, and so on. This means that the library media specialist might need to have some power over what students and teachers have access to and what they can reach online at times. The ever-evolving world of websites and resources is too rich to block as a routine, and overcoming the filters is too tangled in the time-consuming red tape of bypassing permission, a barrier often kept strong by the IT department (which, for the most part, does not work with students). This media needs to live everywhere, and the media specialist's new role is about finding ways to engage the new literacies both inside and outside the library.

New Audiences

Another important component of a modern balanced literacy program is audience. Teachers have traditionally been the only audience for student work, but digital tools and access have given us the opportunity to broaden audiences to a global network of potential collaborators. This is important for two reasons. One, students gain valuable information about their own work by inviting others in to critique and help revise what they've done. This expansion of audience amplifies the learning to include considerations of multiple perspectives that are based on both experience and culture. The second reason is differentiated style. Different audiences demand different ways of presenting information, whether that means writing in a specific way or demonstrating understanding through multimedia presentations. Teachers who help their students expand their audiences are giving them opportunities for enhanced and deeper learning.

CONTINUUM COACH: THE HIGH SCHOOL RESEARCH PAPER

The traditional high school research paper hasn't changed much. Generally speaking, the parameters include the reading and analysis of several texts, stating a thesis, and then supporting it with details. Depending on the teacher, the length is variable, what is valued (grammar and content) is also variable, and the audience is almost always just the teacher. What college or career path does this method prepare students for? They can write a paper, sure, but what requisite skills have they learned? What requisite skills were taught? How does the demand for a work product reflect the instruction or lack thereof?

In terms of the continuum (figure 2.1, page 32), the entry point for the high school research paper is toward the traditional zone. How can we modernize this project with multiple forms of media and multiple modes of presentation and change the audience to one that is global and interactive?

What if the product, the research paper itself, were not the endpoint of instruction? What if the preparation and the after-product exploration were where the real learning happened? How would we measure that? More importantly, what would it really mean for students and their learning? Right now, the formula for learning is to give directions to students, asking them to create a product. That formula is often time dependent, and we're surprised when the learning is variable or the learning represents a continuum within our classrooms from low level to mastery.

What if we made the instruction *learning dependent* instead of *time dependent*? What if time became the variable? Then, a student may reach the learning finish line earlier or later, but the learning itself becomes constant (Buffum, Mattos, & Weber, 2009). The shift of emphasis sends a message that quality work is important and opens the doors to expanding the learning by inviting audience participation to enrich the product.

For the research paper, think of the middle ring of a bull's-eye as the product, the center ring as the preparation zone, and the outer ring as the new audience zone. More learning happens in the preparation and audience zones, the inner and outer rings, than in the product zone. Based on the continuum, the product is on the traditional end.

We can upgrade every part of this. In the preparation zone, students need access to relevant and useful information. In fact,

Continued →

we would say this is a good time for students to start defending what they are doing or finding—even before they defend their thesis statements. They should be able to articulate and rationalize the inclusion of some information and media over other bits of information, even if initially they find a plethora of media on their chosen topic.

They should have opportunities to discuss this information and its relevance with multiple audiences: the other students, the teacher, other schools around the country, and other students around the world. This can be done through physical conversations and with web tools such as blogs, online noteboards, microblogs such as Twitter, or live video feeds. There are literally hundreds of interactive tools for this purpose to choose from on the web.

Students could engage in collaborative prewriting through a tool like Google Drive, while attending to the close reading of texts and media that they will analyze. When it comes time to shift to individual work, students can write in a multitude of ways using a variety of tools that include both print and digital. The whole process is collaborative and transparent, which makes it *googleproof*—that is, it avoids copied-and-pasted jobs.

Once the product is complete (as a step in the research paper process rather than the end assessment moment), students move into the audience zone, not only preparing a multimedia presentation of their work but also sharing it with multiple audiences for feedback. As the feedback comes in—in the form of comments on a YouTube video, interactions on a blog, or conversations within other web tools—students revise and edit their work accordingly. Grading could be based on their levels of participation in all parts of the process rather than the product itself, perhaps with a rubric that students develop collaboratively. In the 21st century, amplifying the work to multiple audiences allows students to experience new perspectives, to have access to edits and revisions they may not have considered, and to collaborate on a global level.

Close Reading

As students move into intermediate grades and secondary classrooms, *guided reading* becomes *close reading*, which supports students as they move into textual analysis and interpretation. Close reading is not an all-the-time strategy, but it is important enough to be included as a component of effective literacy instruction in a balanced literacy model. Close reading is specifically about keeping the reader focused on the text, asking and answering text-based questions, and inferring and drawing conclusions based on claims and specific evidence from the text.

While close reading is not a new strategy, schools are working to include more of this practice to meet the expectations of the new Common Core standards (NGA & CCSSO, 2010), including the following (Fisher & Frey, 2012):

- **Complex texts**—Teachers identify complex texts using a variety of methods, including quantitative (Lexile measures), qualitative (rubrics), and reader and task considerations.

- **Rereadings**—Students have multiple opportunities to reread the text, both in full and through the use of selected lines or paragraphs as they relate to questions or discussions.

- **Short passages or short excerpts from longer works**—Rereading is one practice of close reading. For longer texts, this rereading can be from several specific paragraphs chosen by the teacher to help make connections around big ideas or essential thematic elements.

- **Limited prereadings**—Students should just jump in and read. It may be necessary to frontload a vocabulary word or two, but close reading is largely done as *cold reading*—that is, reading a text that has not been read before and one that has not had a lot of preteaching associated with it.

- **Annotations**—Highlighting, underlining, and taking in-text notations are helpful during close reading. Additionally, students can use more modern forms of annotation like collaborative online writing tools, survey tools, note-taking tools, and apps that aid in the collaborative collection of student notes, connections, claims, evidence, and conclusions.

- **Text-dependent questions**—Ask students to go back into the text and find specific evidence to support their reasoning or conclusions. Rather than students giving opinion-type answers with little or no support or metacognition around what led them to think what they are thinking, close reading demands a higher level of rigor, asking students to be reading detectives who gather evidence and draw conclusions based on the evidence.

The goal of a traditional balanced literacy program is to engage students in literacy practices and continually nudge them to the next level of sophistication in order to ensure proficiency in reading and writing. And as we continue this work, we must also raise the bar if we are to take students to the rigorous levels expected by the Common Core standards, provincial standards, or standards anywhere that demand higher levels of depth and rigor. Moreover, the traditional components of balanced literacy must be expanded to include modern tools, modern processes, and online and face-to-face collaboration. Additionally, progress monitoring within an expanded definition of what proficiency looks like in our modern world must be clear for students and teachers right through the high school level. This will ensure that that sophisticated levels of engagement in authentic and novel work is the goal, enabling students to achieve independence and proficiency in college- and career-ready work.

Modern Instructional Commitments

To successfully integrate new tools, devices, and Internet resources into everyday classroom use with young students, teachers need to include the tools on a consistent and routine basis, the same way classrooms have used books and composition notebooks in the past. Many classrooms have several desktop computers in the room. Students need to use these stations every day, perhaps by alternating turns to ensure equity of access.

For example, teachers typically ask K–2 students in the emergent stages of literacy to write a journal entry as an independent activity. A small group of them could work on computers or tablets each day while others write on paper. The purpose of the task is always to express meaning in print—even in kindergarten. Some children will print or write in manuscript form, while others will type on the keyboard. Ubiquitous access to modern literacy tools, such as class computers, creates a consistent routine in literacy work, rather than being an "event" (such as bringing in the mobile cart), and this regularity will ensure that even if there aren't enough computers or devices for everyone, all students will have access in a systematic way.

Until a 1:1 ratio of devices is the norm in our classrooms, we must use the tools systematically and with more equity. That way, just as students at the kindergarten level learn about directionality when they write, they will also learn to log onto the computer, connect to their folder on the school network, write, and save their "written work" in their digital folder on their school server. *Automaticity*, which means moving new learning into action that requires little thought, will soon emerge in the same way that young students go online, log onto email or the network, connect with loved ones and experts via Skype, and publish writing to various places on the web. Automaticity comes with practice, and consistent practice must be built into the everyday classroom work.

For this work to happen on a consistent basis, the tools must be housed in the classroom. When teachers have to schedule use of the computer cart and make an appointment to build in modern work, the immersive experience is lost. Whether a small bank of desktop computers lives in the room or a combination of tablets, computers, and mobile devices is always available, these literacy tools must be regular classroom features. Teachers move their instruction along at a brisk pace, and if devoting time to getting everyone logged onto machines becomes a special and time-consuming event, planning such events will move down that teacher's list of priorities in the future. Finding and removing barriers and frustration that can slow the immersion of modern work will take leaders who are connected, who can listen, and who can plan strategically with clear expectations in mind. Twenty-first century students are immersed in technology from very early ages; often, the only time they are not is when they are in school. Pulling them out of their known world to learn in the context of a nonimmersive world is akin to expecting a fish to thrive in the desert.

Administrative Missions

All of what we've shared so far is dependent on access—access to materials, both print and digital; access to the Internet; and access to digital devices that support it all. To build the vision of what could and should be in place in an engaging and modern literacy program, school leaders must be aware of what the new literacies are, and they must be involved in creating a vision and mission to help their school venture into new literacy territories.

School leaders and IT directors must work with teachers and students to provide the access classrooms need while considering the safety of the school network. It is challenging to keep up with the innovations that technology has made possible, but it is up to the adults in the system to continue to learn in order to keep up with what students will be exposed to. For many, both the learning curve and the stakes remain high. Adults must possess a level of proficiency that prepares them to manage new methods of instruction. Collaborative planning and an articulated curriculum need to be in place to help students see positive ways to use these tools and diminish the potential for the negative behaviors that can take place in cyberspace.

Many schools have equipped classrooms with interactive whiteboards that allow teachers to use online tools and websites that include instructional strategies beyond the textbook. Teachers' proficiencies with new instructional methods may be increasing, but we must work to be sure that these proficiencies move to include our students as well. *They* must be consuming and producing with new tools, not just the teacher. If students merely sit and watch instruction on a whiteboard instead of a blackboard, this is not progress. The visuals may be better, but the ownership of learning remains in the teacher's hands.

Educators must have honest conversations about their beliefs concerning what schools should be offering students. The adults under the school roof must work together to build the vision for the immediate future and then work strategically to put the necessary steps in place, with support of the community and outside organizations. Constituents from all groups, including the students, must be present and ready to shape and support the needed changes, including decisions about access to school networks and in-school use of cell phones—policies that schools routinely challenge.

A white paper titled "Funding the Shift to Digital Learning" suggests a variety of ways to use funding sources and bring your own device (BYOD) models to help make digital integration a reality in our schools (Bailey, Schneider, & Vander Ark, 2012). Authors John Bailey, Carri Schneider, and Tom Vander Ark (2012) point out that "most states and districts will deploy mixed methods that blend elements of state, district, parent, and student contributions in combination with practices that leverage existing financial resources and reallocate dollars inside current budgets" (p. 10).

We might also calculate and analyze the amount of money we are spending to fund the standardized testing processes many schools are tied to and possibly redirect these monies to help fund the modernization of our schools. The high-stakes testing culture that most schools are working hard to manage is overwhelmed with pencil-and-paper tests. As long as these objective pencil-and-paper tests define the value of our schools, instruction will be hard-pressed to move away from preparing for them and the traditional literacy they measure.

Creating modern, multimodal assessments that represent both modern literacy and future-forward preparation has the potential to move our schools into a new era, but it will take collaboration from those in and out of school to make it a reality. A change in assessments will drive a change in instruction. Thoughtful, interactive, integrated, and high-level performance-based assessments are possible with new literacies, but we must build capacity in those working in our schools to move in that direction. Policymakers must be open to such change, and listening to feedback from the field on ways to include more authentic, performance-based assessments must be included as part of the feedback loop that should be the goal of all assessment.

As a global community of educators, we need to be clear that the purpose of creating a school program is to prepare students for the future world they are entering, rather than holding educators accountable for and hostage to the practices of the past.

Strategic Action Planning

Establishing an effective team to modernize the literacy work of the school will require a distributed and shared leadership approach. As Jim Collins (2001) reminds us in his article "Good to Great," getting the right people on the bus is one of the first actions a good leader will take when forming a committee to help steer high-level work.

> Leaders of companies that go from good to great start not with "where" but with "who." They start by getting the right people on the bus, the wrong people off the bus, and the right people in the right seats. And they stick with that discipline—first the people, then the direction—no matter how dire the circumstances.

Once an effective team is in place, team members should begin to develop a vision and action plans. Team members should be representative of the school community and can begin to serve as resources by building capacity in the faculty. The team should gather data to audit the practices that are already in place and solicit input from teachers regarding attitudes and struggles that may be slowing the current energy to upgrade the classroom work. Strong administrative support is critical, yet the knowledge and vision for the work will exist in many aspects of the organization. The team leader or leaders do not have to be the administrators in the school, but the administrator's input and support are critical elements to the success of the effort. Building and district leadership positions are often not as long-term as they have been in the past; thus, shared leadership will not be dependent on only one or two people. Team leaders should help to organize and facilitate meetings, and the group should begin to meet, communicate, and lead, using the very same modern tools they expect all teachers and students will begin to use.

Once the team is established, developing a common language around modern literacy concepts to enable clear discussion about the work using common vocabulary is important. This team will in turn extend those understandings to other teachers and staff members. The team should then develop a vision for the work, and the vision should focus not on the tools but on the outcomes of high-level literacy work for the world students will enter. The tools will change; the high-level, connected, and interactive 21st century work will remain.

Teams need to outline actionable and measurable steps in the scope of the larger picture of curriculum and vision. They may list action steps for many overlapping areas, depending on where the school is with current practice, and each of these implementation plans will typically require leadership, professional development, communication, and time. Teams will accomplish some steps more quickly than others. They may simply need to formalize some to become nonnegotiables. For example, a policy like "All students in grades K–5 will use a computer or device each week to write within a variety of formats" can be put in place quickly. Other goals require a longer range plan, such as a 1:1 device implementation for tablets, laptops, or other digital tools. Table 2.1 shows a possible template for outlining the action plans.

Table 2.1: Outlining an Action Plan

Topic	Action
Curricular area and action step	What content area will be the focus? What specific steps will you take?
Lead person or group	Who will be the lead person or group to facilitate the actions? What other group or member roles need to be defined?
Date and time frame	What is a reasonable deadline? When will the planning and implementation take place?
Budget and resources	What resources will we need? Is a budget necessary for the action?
Implementation and professional development	Before implementation, is there a need for professional development? Does the professional development require in-house support or an outside consultant? What are the action steps?
Evidence and reflection	What evidence should we look for to know we met our goal? What questions do we need to ask to modify this for future implementations?

Examining the existing literacy curriculum is critical to knowing where upgrades are possible, and if the existing curriculum is weak, schools must tackle this issue first. Trying to upgrade and modernize a literacy curriculum that doesn't exist will not take the work in a good direction. High-priced devices will engage students in activities, but this is not something schools can necessarily afford. Schools must first articulate the outcomes for a 21st century student, and the rest can follow.

Find the expertise that exists under your school roof and work with those staff members to plan both professional development sessions with teachers and curriculum facilitation work with groups. Key people must be included in the strategic planning and reflection work, including students, parents, and the information technology department. Share a formal plan with all stakeholders and use this plan to promote the new literacy work, as well as the action steps in which the school will be involved. A key point to communicate to stakeholders is that the work in progress will require revision and adjustments as time passes. Schools should share successes and openly discuss challenges that arise with the expectation that everyone can be part of the solutions. Collect feedback from those involved in the implementation and display status documents to keep everyone in the loop. Recognizing those who contribute to the work and celebrating the successes, both large and small, will help sustain the momentum that moves the modern literacy program forward.

Conclusion

In *Fahrenheit 451*, Ray Bradbury (1953) explores the notion of a singular media source as an easier and more efficient mode of communication and expression. In the story, books are burned as unnecessary anachronisms that only get people thinking—reminiscent of the logic of keeping slaves uneducated so they won't ask questions about lives that could be better—a topic explored by Frederick Douglass (1845) a century before Bradbury.

While we don't want to suggest that setting the traditional on fire in favor of modern processes is the right thing to do, we do want to reiterate that singular modes no longer work for the modern thinking world we live in. Literacy in any form should not be about indoctrination and linear actions; it should be inclusive, expansive, interconnected, and fluid—a continuum of opportunities that represent multiple versions of receptive and expressive communication across multiple literacy access points.

It's inappropriate to continue to discuss what 21st century is without any attendant action. To be honest, everything we are advocating for in these pages needed to have been put in place yesterday. Evolution does not regress. Whatever is improved on is passed to the next generation. Instruction should be an amalgam of everything we've learned about learning, but instead, it largely represents comfort zones of the past. We have been entrusted with students who need us to stop discussing the need to move on. We must get up and lead the way now.

Our students are already engaging in modern literacy practice. They are comfortable living in a digital universe where they receive vast amounts of information. They are skilled at remixing this information in multiple media formats, and they've even created their own codes for distilling our language down to what amounts to digital shorthand (such as LOL and OMG). What they aren't skilled at is discerning the relevance of information for a task or solving a problem in nonlinear formats. They rarely make intended connections and simply collate information as part of a checklist that represents *doing* more than *learning*.

Modern literacy instruction is vital for preparing students for the 21st century world, whether it's for a career or for higher education. Teachers are the modern literacy "evolutioneers," building physical and digital bridges to the future so that our students, our children, can communicate and learn in more effective ways that matter to our time and theirs. Teachers who understand the modern landscape are essential for guiding students through all of the modern resources to which we now have access. They are the guides on the sides, curation coaches, and filters for access to information in the modern world. Our brave new world of literacy possibilities allows so many opportunities for constructing what modern literacy will ultimately be. We know that we have to consider the continuum, the landscape of what is accessed, connected, and learned. We know that foundations are still important and that they are the seeds for literate digital natives. We know that in the 21st century, literacy is limitless, expansive, and constantly changing. We have reached the event horizon of modern literacy. There is no going back.

References and Resources

Allington, R. L. (1977). If they don't read much, how they ever gonna get good? *Journal of Reading, 21*, 57–61.

Allington, R. L. (2009). *What really matters in response to intervention: Research-based designs.* Boston: Allyn & Bacon.

Bailey, J., Schneider, C., & Vander Ark, T. (2012, August). *Funding the shift to digital learning: Three strategies for funding sustainable high-access environments.* Accessed at http://digitallearningnow.com/wp-content/uploads/2012/08/DLN-Smart -Series-Paper-1-Final.pdf on April 12, 2013.

Bilton, N. (2010). *I live in the future and here's how it works: Why your world, work, and brain are being creatively disrupted.* New York: Crown Business.

Bradbury, R. (1953). *Fahrenheit 451.* New York: Ballantine Books.

Buffum, A., Mattos, M., & Weber, C. (2009). *Pyramid response to intervention: RTI, professional learning communities, and how to respond when kids don't learn.* Bloomington, IN: Solution Tree Press.

Calkins, L., Ehrenworth, M., & Lehman, C. (2012). *Pathways to the common core: Accelerating achievement.* Portsmouth, NH: Heinemann.

Collins, J. (2001, October). *Good to great.* Accessed at www.jimcollins.com/article _topics/articles/good-to-great.html on June 26, 2013.

Douglass, F. (1845). *Narrative of the life of Frederick Douglass.* Cambridge: Harvard University Press.

Fisher, D., & Frey, N. (2012). *Engaging the adolescent learner: Text complexity and close readings.* (1st ed., Vol. 1). Newark, DE: International Reading Association. Accessed at www.reading.org/Libraries/members-only/Fisher_and_Frey_-_Text _Complexity_-_January_2012.pdf on February 9, 2013.

Fisher, M. (2012a, September 25). Literacy: Solution fluency [Web log post]. Accessed at http://smartblogs.com/education/2012/09/25/solution-fluency on October 24, 2012.

Fisher, M. (2012b, June 29). Snapshot of a modern learner [Web log post]. Accessed at http://smartblogs.com/education/2012/06/29/snapshot-modern-learner/ on November 11, 2012.

Fountas, I. C., & Pinnell, G. S. (1996). *Guided reading: Good first teaching for all children.* Portsmouth, NH: Heinemann.

Guthrie, J. T., Wigfield, A., & You, W. (2012). Instructional contexts for engagement and achievement in reading. In S. L. Christenson, A. L. Reschly, & C. Wylie (Eds.), *Handbook of research on student engagement* (pp. 601–634). New York: Springer.

Hsia, L. (2011, November 17). How transmedia storytelling is changing TV [Web log post]. Accessed at http://mashable.com/2011/11/17/transmedia-tv on July 12, 2012.

Jenkins, H. (2008). *Convergence culture: Where old and new media collide.* New York: NYU Press.

Krashen, S. (2004). *The power of reading: Insights from the research* (2nd ed.). New York: Libraries Unlimited.

Lehmann, C. (Producer). (2009, March 28). Joe's Non-Netbook [Web Video]. Accessed at www.youtube.com/watch?v=SkhpmEZWuRQ on October 22, 2013.

National Governors Association Center for Best Practices & Council of Chief State School Officers. (2010). *Common Core State Standards for English language arts and literacy in history/social studies, science, & technical subjects.* Washington, DC: Authors.

Pearson, P. D. (2004). The reading wars. *Educational Policy, 18*(1), 216–252.

Reyhner, J. (2008). *The reading wars.* Accessed at http://jan.ucc.nau.edu/~jar /Reading_Wars.html on April 19, 2013.

Ann Ward Johnson, PhD, is an independent consultant who works extensively in schools and organizations internationally on implementing Mapping to the Core (MTTC), assessment, Curriculum 21 upgrades, and the new literacies in their curriculum. She also trains building and district leaders in using digital applications and in the development of comprehensive implementation plans. Her practical approach to design and alignment is based on her experience as a classroom teacher, associate superintendent, principal, and adjunct professor.

She and Heidi Hayes Jacobs outline the four phases of quality curriculum design in their book *The Curriculum Mapping Planner: Templates, Tools, and Resources for Effective Professional Development*. Ann is also coauthor of the LivePlanner, a professional development companion to *Mapping to the Core: Integrating the Common Core Standards Into Your Local School Curriculum*.

To learn more about Ann's work, visit her website, http://annjohnson.net, or follow her on Twitter @annwjohnson.

Bill Sheskey, MA, is the director of instructional technology for the Charlotte-Mecklenburg Schools in Charlotte, North Carolina, and a Curriculum 21 faculty team member. He is a lifetime educator with experience as a school district instructional technology specialist, classroom teacher, and athletic coach. Bill designs and facilitates a series of engaging workshops for educators at international, national, state, and local education conferences that provide participants with interactive tools to engage in the upgrade of curriculum. These dynamic experiences for all levels of educators provide hands-on experience in the development of authentic assessment strategies, essential question writing, and the use of web 2.0 tools. His writing focuses on connecting with tech-savvy students and engaging them with the communication tools that they use in their daily lives.

Bill is a contributing author to Heidi Hayes Jacobs's *Curriculum 21: An Essential Education for a Changing World*. To learn more about Bill's work, follow him on Twitter @billsheskey.

To book Ann Ward Johnson or Bill Sheskey for professional development, contact pd@solution-tree.com.

Chapter 3

Entry Points for Leading and Implementing the New Literacies

By Ann Ward Johnson and Bill Sheskey

The number of districts in the United States planning to distribute tablets or other new mobile devices to students continues to multiply. Do teachers have the training they need to be successful at using them to enhance instruction in the classroom?

We bring to this chapter two different perspectives. Bill, a veteran teacher, coach, and supervisor, is very comfortable with technology and learning new tools, and Ann, a veteran teacher, administrator, and professional development (PD) director, uses the tools in the classroom and workshop settings when training teachers and administrators. Our intent in writing this chapter is to share specific examples from the field, implementation strategies, and possible entry points for schools to use when they start implementing the new literacies. Hopefully, if you have already started to implement the new literacies, our suggestions will support your work and help you consider other possibilities.

One of the important themes in this chapter is the empowerment of school leaders through user-friendly applications in order to move professional development beyond the traditional teacher workday training session. The growth of Facebook, Twitter, and texting and the increased capabilities of cell phones have had a revolutionary impact on communication methods in all demographic areas of society. School leaders are now responsible for leading and communicating with web-based tools that we use in a social network context. School leaders also have the opportunity to model and use simple web-based applications as leadership tools to reinforce the basic skills of writing and presentation and to demonstrate higher-order thinking skills.

Technology-Inspired PD

When Bill was working as an instructional technology specialist in the school district of Oconee County, South Carolina, superintendent Valerie Truesdale approached him with this question: "What do we need in our classrooms to immediately upgrade the instructional technology capabilities for the teachers?"

The district had just accessed the new on-demand video service from Discovery Education called United Streaming, a move away from the traditional VCR and television for delivering media to the classroom. The teachers were very excited about the fact that they could pull up resources from Discovery Education instantly and use the media clips that were already aligned to state standards. While teachers had at least one desktop computer in each classroom, they lacked a way to project images from the computer to a large screen for classroom viewing. A computer projector cost around $900, and to install them in over five hundred classrooms was a significant expense that the school would need to justify to the school board. And Valerie did not want to install the projectors in the classrooms without first training teachers in how to use them effectively to create enhanced learning opportunities.

Bill designed a twelve-hour professional development course divided into three four-hour after-school sessions. The district received approval, ordered the projectors ahead of time, and had them ready to connect in the classrooms.

The leadership team learned quickly that the teachers were highly motivated to earn the projectors by taking the training class, and despite the fact that there was no extra pay, the classes filled immediately. The incentives were the projector and the twelve recertification credit hours. The training was very practical, focusing only on strategies and applications that teachers could use in their classrooms immediately.

Following the four trainings, the school district distributed over five hundred projectors for classrooms in two years. Over the next five years, they moved on to Flip cameras, MP3 players, and web cameras as incentives for a variety of professional development experiences for the teachers. The district built classroom webpages, designed digital storytelling platforms, and explored myriad web 2.0 tools for learning.

This method of distributing instructional hardware into classrooms was the impetus for creating a new form of professional development. Teachers were going to have the opportunity to use tools and applications in the classroom that up until that time had been visible only on a small computer screen. The classroom projector screens were wonderful for engaging students in the on-demand video sources, web content, and interactive websites that were emerging at that time. The changes were exciting; teachers were now seeking professional development on how to access, categorize, and prioritize all these various applications.

Of course, new technology alone will not guarantee success. The integration of technology should not occur for its own sake. Teachers and educators require structured and relevant professional development to support the integration of a multitude of learning applications that are available now.

Getting Started in the New Literacies

We have organized our chapter around examples that highlight the ways various schools have started the process of upgrading units through the integration of the new literacies. After each example, we identify specific steps used in the training, so readers can replicate them. Following the implementation steps, we include resources for each example. These are merely starting points. As we are well aware, the available resources are constantly evolving and changing. Following the resources, we indicate some additional entry points—other possible ways to begin the work in a school or district—that we hope readers will consider.

Not all educators have the same degree of comfort and aptitude when it comes to incorporating technology into their daily teaching practice. In this first example, we look at applications that use hardware already in place in a classroom and are already aligned with standards. This district experienced success because of the small number of applications and its focus on showing how teachers could use them to upgrade very specific lessons, units, and assignments.

Field Example: Digital Literacy

While working with a large school system in the Kansas City, Missouri, area on upgrading curriculum maps with digital applications, we worked with a leadership cohort that had little experience using web 2.0 applications to increase communication and the exchange of information. Another roadblock they faced was the restrictive Internet filtering system in the district, which discouraged the use of interactive web 2.0 applications. Keeping this in mind, we began by sharing an easy-to-use, nonfiltered web 2.0 application, TodaysMeet, for creating an instant message board that participants could use to share ideas during the session. The participants were prompted to examine their existing curriculum maps and identify an application they could infuse into their unit maps to upgrade learning.

We were both modeling the use of an application and effectively guiding the group on how teachers could use it themselves when leading upgrade sessions. We explained that web 2.0 applications don't require email registrations and do not have paid advertising that might cause the Internet filtering system to block them. The group immediately saw the value of using the message board to share information during the upgrade process.

In the next activity, we shared an application that a school leader or leadership team could use to create a webpage for leading an ongoing professional development initiative. At that point, you could feel the excitement in the room. The teams could see how they could use web 2.0 digital applications as communication tools as they worked with staff to upgrade their curriculum. They were now motivated to begin the process of upgrading their own digital literacy skills to successfully lead their school faculties.

When school leaders and leadership teams facilitate a professional development session or even just a weekly faculty meeting, they face the challenge of managing a group of people who may be distracted and checking email, text messaging, or searching online. The challenges are similar to those that classroom teachers face with students who multitask with their smartphones. In all workshops with school leaders, we use back channels, audience response, and polling applications to engage teachers and administrators in whatever professional development we are conducting. Polling tools like Poll Everywhere or Mentimeter are a good way to distribute essential questions prior to a faculty meeting, so the team leader can share responses when the meeting starts, thus quickly engaging the participants. Reducing the meeting time will also make you a popular leader!

Implementation Steps

The implementation steps for this field example were as follows:

1. We designed a two-day workshop that focused on upgrading curriculum maps and units using web 2.0 applications for curriculum coordinators, teacher leaders, and assistant principals in charge of curriculum from schools across the system. We tested the web 2.0 applications in the district's filtering system prior to the workshop.

2. Grade-level teams brainstormed how one unit could be upgraded with web 2.0 applications. On the first day, we directed the group to the Curriculum 21 Clearinghouse of digital applications (www.curriculum21.com/clearinghouse) and provided two hours of grade-level targeted exploration of applications that they could use as unit upgrades.

3. We set up a message board (http://todaysmeet.com) and prompted the group to use it to share its search results. At the end of the exploring activity, we copied the posts in the message board and pasted them into an electronic document that they could share with the entire group.

4. On the second day, the leadership teams constructed a simple website using Yola (www.yola.com). In the process of building this site, each team built its own custom clearinghouse for the specific web 2.0 applications that they had selected for their unit upgrades.

Other Possible Entry Points

Two other possible entry points are student response systems like Socrative and Twitter.

Student Response Systems

The English language arts (ELA) teachers we worked with at our summer conference used online quizzes for quick formative assessment. The ones they had used, however, allowed only for multiple-choice responses, and they wanted to incorporate higher-level questions for their students. We shared Socrative (http://socrative.com), developed at the Massachusetts Institute of Technology. It is a smart student response system that empowers teachers to engage their classrooms through a series of assessment exercises and games via smartphones, laptops, and tablets. A variety of question levels include the open-ended text responses that the English language arts teachers were looking for.

Twitter

Samantha Miller (2012) describes fifty ways to use Twitter in the classroom, including writing poetry, telling stories, becoming politically active, facilitating research, connecting with other classrooms, and following current events—all in 140 characters or less! Because Twitter is blocked in most school districts, teachers can substitute TodaysMeet to provide a safe and easy-to-use writing application for any content area.

Resources

A variety of resources are available to educators to support their work in integrating digital literacy.

- **Web application**: Curriculum 21 Clearinghouse (www.curriculum21 .com/clearinghouse)
- **Meeting board:** TodaysMeet (http://todaysmeet.com)
- **Simple website builders:**
  - Yola (www.yola.com)
  - Weebly (http://weebly.com)
  - Wix (http://wix.com)
- **Student response system:** Socrative (http://socrative.com)
- **Instant polling:** Mentimeter (http://mentimeter.com)
- **Higher-level polls, quizzes, and open-ended responses:** InfuseLearning (http://infuselearning.com)

Field Example: Media Literacy

We had the opportunity to work in two small city districts in Georgia that were looking for multimedia resources easily accessible to teachers and safe for students. We designed a hands-on professional development workshop that guided teachers in the upgrade of curriculum units and assessments using web-based media sources that had been previously reviewed and were content-area specific. These sessions focused on upgrading writing and research applications that would engage students in a variety of literacy activities. We began with the Khan Academy, a free, online collection of over 3,500 educational video lectures, tutorials, and activities that cover the core K–12 content areas. The teachers examined their existing units to look for entry points for the Khan Academy content and learning activities.

One of the workshop sessions was a half-day training that guided teachers in the design of writing prompts for ELA and social studies, resource collection for science and mathematics labs, and the use of library and museum resources that Internet filters did not block. The target for this activity was to coach teachers through the process of upgrading curriculum units they had used in the past with digital media applications.

The mathematics and science teachers in the group expressed the desire for the most up-to-date content-area resources. The examination of NeoK12, TeacherTube, iTunes U, and the Khan Academy provided the mathematics and science teachers with rich and relevant resources for curriculum upgrades. This group then began the process of categorizing and creating tables in a document to organize resources into subgroups for specific units.

In our professional development experiences around the United States and Canada, we have learned that teachers are hungry for new forms of media resources to upgrade their curriculum and assessments. The wide-open YouTube–type resources have too many security issues to permit their use as learning tools in the K–12 school setting. Teachers are looking for resources that are safe for student use.

Implementation Steps

The implementation steps for this field example were as follows:

1. We grouped ELA teachers into grade-level teams and directed them to a number of writing prompts for their students. We shared three prompts—Education Northwest, Creativity Portal, and OneWord—all excellent resources for providing new ideas that will help students over that difficult step of developing an idea on which to write. The ELA group shared other media resources to stimulate the writing process and shared them with their colleagues on the TodaysMeet message board.

2. Social studies teachers searched for primary sources on the American Memory webpage of the United States Library of Congress (http://memory .loc.gov) that students could examine for their historical value and for their relevance to events they're studying in class. The teachers also visited museum websites from all over the world that offered authentic, up-to-date research applications for student writing and media projects.

3. The mathematics and science teachers explored the most modern applications for upgrading content in their curriculum. Using the mathematics and science search engine WolframAlpha (www.wolframalpha.com), teachers upgraded the content-specific search skills with their students.

4. The teachers shared their experiences with the Khan Academy after using it with students. This was scheduled as a post-workshop activity board that was sent via email to the entire group using TodaysMeet.

Other Possible Entry Points

Other possible entry points for using the new literacies are infomercials, how-to videos, and lab reports.

Infomercials

In a Des Moines, Iowa, area high school, all of the teachers received Apple MacBooks. The iMovie video-editing software included with the laptops is a powerful and highly engaging tool enabling teachers to easily create their own digital movies. Each content-area department created its own sixty-second infomercial about the course offerings available to students. The teachers enjoyed this activity, and a natural level of competitiveness emerged that raised the quality of the infomercials. In the PC environment, students can produce infomercials using Windows Movie Maker or a web-based video editing tool called Magisto (www.magisto.com).

How-To Videos

In a professional development session with preK–5 media specialists in South Carolina's Beaufort County Schools, we facilitated the development of how-to videos to teach students how to do research in the media center. The media specialist used Windows Movie Maker, an easy-to-use program on computers that run Windows 7, Windows 8, and Windows XP. With minimal training, the media specialists collaborated to make videos on everything from how to research periodicals to media center etiquette. They then uploaded the videos to the media center.

Lab Reports

In a professional development session, middle school science teachers in Chicago created a lesson that prompted students to do one science lab report per semester using a digital media production tool. The teachers guided students in the process of presenting the results of a lab report in a video format. These students did not have access to iMovie or Movie Maker, so we shared WeVideo, an online platform for collaborative video production. It has the basic editing tools for simple media production, and everything is stored online so students can access their projects from any computer with an Internet connection. The students then critiqued their peers' lab reports using the computer in the classroom.

Resources

Here are some other resources educators can use for infomercials, how-to videos, and lab reports.

- **Content-area resources:**
  - The Khan Academy (http://khanacademy.org)

- NeoK12 (www.neok12.com)
- TeacherTube (www.teachertube.com)
- iTunes U (www.apple.com/education/itunes-u)
- **Movie-making tools:**
  - WeVideo (www.wevideo.com)
  - Windows Movie Maker (http://windows.microsoft.com/en-us /windows-live/movie-maker)
  - Magisto (www.magisto.com)
  - iMovie (www.apple.com/ilife/imovie)
- **Mathematics and science search engine:** WolframAlpha (www .wolframalpha.com)
- **Meeting board:** TodaysMeet (http://todaysmeet.com)
- **Primary and museum sources:**
  - September 11, 2001 (http://archive.org/details/911)
  - Library of Congress Teachers (www.loc.gov/teachers)
  - American Memory (http://memory.loc.gov)
  - The King Center (www.thekingcenter.org/archive)
- **Writing prompts:**
  - Education Northwest (http://educationnorthwest.org)
  - Creativity Portal (www.creativity-portal.com/prompts/imagination .prompt.html)
  - OneWord (http://oneword.com)

Field Example: Global Literacy

We trained elementary and middle school principals and teachers in Eastern Pennsylvania to design and construct websites for their schools and classrooms. The motivation for building these sites was to create a web-based portal, so classrooms could join the ePals global network and Skype in the Classroom to connect with other classrooms around the world. These networks are secure for student use and offer large numbers of participants.

There are two parts to this field example. The first is the construction of the school and classroom webpage; the second is the selection of a global network to join.

Creating connections with other schools and classrooms requires a quality website that offers a virtual platform that connects students in, say, Eastern Pennsylvania to students in Auckland or Mangalore. Locally, a class webpage also serves as an academic support resource where parents and students can collaborate in the learning process. By providing access to project and assignment calendars, test schedules, web 2.0 learning, and communication resources, class webpages are valuable communication tools for schools and help parents stay involved in their child's learning process. Globally, the class webpage provides a gateway for visitors and a place for connecting students in programs like ePals and Skype in the Classroom.

At each of the schools, we set up a four-hour session with the teachers and administrators for building web pages. The session opened with a virtual tour of exemplary classroom and school websites that were connected globally. We prompted the group to think like a parent, student, or foreign visitor while looking for information on their own school's website. In addition, we coached teachers on how to use the criteria in the rubric as a guide for evaluating classroom webpages.

In the next part of the training, we divided the school faculty into grade-level teams and prompted them to reach consensus on what they felt were the essential components to include on their classroom webpages. After reviewing the exemplary sites, the teams agreed to include calendars, academic support resources, and links to information about the local culture. Because it is also important to have consistency in design and navigation, the next step was to reach consensus on the format for the resource pages. We modeled how to build them in Microsoft Word using a table. We then gave teachers time to review a variety of formats for the resource pages and to search for at least four web-based resources that would be useful to students and parents. As they found these sites, they created titles and one-sentence descriptions about how to use the sites and added them to their tables.

During the last half of the four-hour session, groups had additional time for website construction; in addition, groups of teachers reviewed ePals and Skype in the Classroom. We prompted the groups to start with either one of these global connection sites and search for classrooms to connect with. The teachers searched by country, grade level, and specific content area. These groups then reported back to the larger group about which global connections they were going to pursue.

One role of the principal in a globally connected school is to coach, guide, and provide a platform for teachers to build quality webpages as an instructional tool. Using the rubric (table 3.1), we coached the principals on how to provide regular

Table 3.1: Rubric for Classroom Websites

Teacher:

Criteria	Exemplary (20 Points)	Proficient (15 Points)	Needs Improvement (10 Points)	Unsatisfactory (5 points)	Total Points
Is the content relevant?	Content is highly informative and provides essential information to students and parents.	Content is informative and provides information to students and parents.	Content is vague and contains little or no information for students and parents.	Contains no content information for students and parents, or contains inaccurate information.	
Is the content up to date?	Information is updated frequently and contains upcoming due dates and assignment information.	Information is somewhat updated and contains some due dates and assignment information.	Information is not up to date and contains few due dates and little assignment information.	Information is not up to date and contains no due dates or assignment information.	
What is the site's appearance and quality (including font, text, and grammar)?	All text is easy to read and well organized and enhances the readability of the site. The site is free from grammatical errors.	Most text is easy to read and the site is well organized. The site contains one grammatical error.	Most text is hard to read and poorly organized. The site contains several grammatical errors.	Text is hard to read and distracts readers from the content. The site contains many grammatical errors.	
What is the quality of the graphics?	All photos, graphics, and videos enhance the content.	Most photos, graphics, and videos enhance the content.	Some photos, graphics, and videos enhance the content.	No photos, graphics, or videos are present.	
How is the site's navigation, and does it contain links?	The site contains internal and external links to educational content. All links connect to the appropriate location.	The site contains some internal and external links to educational content. Most links connect to the appropriate location.	The site contains few internal and external links to educational content. Few of the external links to connecting sites are active.	The site contains no internal or external links to educational content, or the connecting links are not active.	
Total Points					

feedback to the teachers about keeping their webpages up to date and relevant to the current curriculum. When there is an open line of communication with principals about using a webpage as an instructional tool, the teachers' motivation to maintain the class webpage is far greater.

Implementation Steps

The steps for designing and constructing a school or classroom webpage were as follows:

1. We reviewed exemplary classroom webpages using the eduScapes index of existing quality classroom webpages. One example we shared was Oconne County School District in South Carolina. We also shared a rubric that identified specific criteria that teachers could use as a guide for evaluating webpages.

2. After reviewing different classroom and school webpages, the groups brainstormed possible components that could be included on their webpages. They reached consensus on starting with the calendar and the resource page.

3. We then coached teachers in how to build an electronic calendar of classroom activities using easy-to-use applications like Google Calendar and Assign-A-Day. The calendar included major tests, projects, and events that they wanted parents to know about.

4. Since the school did not have the funding to provide a webpage hosting service for teachers and schools, in the next two-hour session teachers and administrators reviewed possible alternatives for a web builder that suited their needs. For simplicity's sake, most teachers use the Yola application, because it is a drag-and-drop system to build text and image areas. Google sites were also popular with the middle school group, because these teachers were comfortable using other Google applications, such as Google Drive, in their work. The teachers practiced linking their electronic calendars to their class webpage and then started building their own clearinghouse of resources to support specific instructional units.

5. We also coached leaders in identifying additional time for their faculty to work in the summer and on teacher workdays so that teachers could build globally connected class pages with the support of other teachers and support staff who had been trained to do so. During this session, we coached leaders in the use of the evaluation rubric and helped them identify questions that aligned to criteria they could use to help coach staff to quality.

6. In an additional two-hour session, administrators and teachers reviewed the instructions for using ePals and Skype in the Classroom and then registered for at least one of them. They then searched ePals and Skype for grade levels and content areas to connect with.

7. Teachers and principals began making initial connections with other educators through ePals and Skype. They asked them questions about their experiences using these networks and about how to make connections to benefit student learning.

Other Possible Entry Points

Other possible entry points for including global literacy are studying country flags and world geography and connecting with authors around the world.

Studying Country Flags and World Geography

The fifth-grade teachers at an independent school in Florida connected with other schools around the world to study the flags of other nations. The teachers were trained in how to use Skype in the Classroom. Students used the live video connection to share the history and symbolism of their country's flag.

Connecting With Authors Around the World

The media specialist in a rural high school in upstate South Carolina used Skype an Author to connect with the authors of summer reading assignments for the junior and senior students. Skype an Author uses a previously established and approved Skype connection to authors of interest to students and teachers. The live connection allowed students to ask authors questions about their background and what inspired them to write the books they had just read.

Resources

A number of resources support educators' work in global literacy.

- **Calendar applications:**
  - Google Calendar (http://learn.googleapps.com/calendar)
  - Assign-A-Day (http://assignaday.4teachers.org)
- **Communication networks:**
  - Skype in the Classroom (https://education.skype.com)

- Skype an Author (https://education.skype.com/resources/168-skype
  -an-author)
- ePals Global Community (http://epals.com)
- Curriculum 21 Global Partnership (www.c21hub.com
  /globalpartnership)
- **Quality webpages:**
  - EduScapes teacher webpage (http://eduscapes.com/tap/topic60)
  - School District of Oconee County (www.oconee.k12.sc.us)
- **Website and blogging applications:**
  - Yola (www.yola.com)
  - WordPress (http://wordpress.com)
  - Google Sites (http://sites.google.com)
  - Google Blogger (http://blogger.com)
  - Edublogs (http://edublogs.org)
  - Weebly for Education (http://education.weebly.com)

A Four-Phase Implementation Model

The field examples we have suggested are possible entry points for a school or teacher beginning to implement the new literacies into the local curriculum or classroom. However, while these upgrades are a great way to get started and build confidence, in order to see lasting benefits a school must consider a thoughtful, comprehensive implementation plan, one that aligns with and supports both short- and long-term goals. With systemwide change and full-scale implementation as our focal point, we suggest a four-phase new literacies implementation model based on our experience working with schools across the United States, in Canada, and internationally. This model is based on the four-phase approach to systemic curriculum mapping to support school improvement efforts (Jacobs & Johnson, 2012).

Within each phase are two strands: one focuses on the content required in the **professional development**, and the other focuses on the **organizational framework** or support structure needed to successfully lead the new literacies. These two strands include targeted areas of focus that a leadership team can use in determining the PD staff needs and support structures needed to sustain the work long term (Jacobs & Johnson, 2009). As it considers the training it needs to target, a leadership team can use these areas of focus as a starting point to assess where teachers are in the process. A leadership team might also use the areas of focus we have highlighted under the support structure strand to lay a foundation for leading and developing a systemic plan. In the sections that follow, we will introduce each phase and suggest the areas of focus that align to it. After outlining the model, we suggest sample activities that support the areas of focus in the phases.

Phase I: Laying the Foundation

Phase I of the implementation model focuses on building a strong foundation on which to sustain the work long term. Here, the professional development aims at deepening a staff's understanding of new literacies, their purpose, and the value they add to the curriculum. The content targeted in the support structure, on the other hand, helps a team consider how to organize itself to ensure success. We have found in our work in curriculum mapping and Mapping to the Core that schools frequently encounter resistance when they don't take time to lay a strong foundation. Leaders encounter confusion from staff when there is a lack of clarity about the new literacies and why they should be integrating them. With this in mind, we have outlined the critical areas of focus for each strand.

Professional Development Content

The following content is included in the professional development for Laying the Foundation:

- Definition of the new literacies—digital, media, and global
- Establishment of purpose and rationale for integrating the new literacies
- Concrete examples of applications of each literacy
- Examples and exploration of types of literacy applications
- Connections with and alignment to other school improvement initiatives

Support Structure

The following are key areas of focus for schools forming an organizational structure to support the implementation of the new forms of literacy:

- Formation of the leadership team to lead the training
- Development of a shared vision
- Identification of short- and long-term goals
- Determination of evidence of success upon completion of the goals

- Commitment to upgrades

- Development of a short-term implementation plan

- Implementation of school policies that ensure integration of the new literacy into the curriculum and technology support

The following field example underscores the importance of the two strands in this phase of the model.

Field Example

Our team had the opportunity to work with Melissa Christie, director of curriculum and instruction for Santa Clara County Office of Education. Melissa was interested in training schools in her county during a summer institute. She originally requested training in Curriculum 21, focusing on the new literacies. However, as we talked, we developed a plan that merged the school's initial work on Mapping to the Core (MTTC) with the new literacies. By doing this, we made a connection between the new literacies and the MTTC curriculum design process.

In order to establish a strong foundation, we trained the county leadership team prior to the summer training. Melissa had recently taken over the role of director and saw this as an opportunity to have her newly formed team collaborate on developing a shared vision while deepening their understanding of the process. Through this collaborative effort, we were able to model how MTTC could serve as the link or connector for the integration of new literacies.

In addition to laying the foundation in MTTC and the new literacies, Melissa's team also saw the importance of working on its support structure. They began by clarifying the purpose of the team and defining its roles and responsibilities. Through the discussion of mapping as a connector for integrating the new literacies, the team crystalized its vision for the project and worked toward identifying both short- and long-term goals. Embedded in the vision was the team's commitment to model upgrades and address the policies and protocols it needed in place to support the work. This initial work served as a skeletal structure and provided the filter through which to make decisions.

Phase II: Launching the Process

This is often where schools start—meaning they skip right to *doing*. However, taking the time to lay a strong foundation in phase I helps teachers more clearly understand the *whats* and *whys*, so they are prepared to work through the process of creating and designing new learning opportunities for their students. In phase

II, the leadership team focuses on the aspects of implementation that ensure quality and engage staff in the process.

Professional Development Content

The following is a list of content that should be included in the professional development as schools transition to the Launching the Process phase:

- Integration of the new literacies in classroom units
- Alignment to the CCSS standards or to any new standards that may be developed, such as global competencies
- Alignment to other unit elements—big ideas, essential questions, content, skills, and assessments
- Implementation of the read-through or review process to determine sequencing of the new literacies and address gaps and repetitions
- Inclusion of coaching strategies to ensure quality upgrades

Support Structure

As schools work to strengthen their support structure for the implementation of the new forms of literacy, they should consider the following:

- Development of protocol for integration of upgrades
- Creation of a coaching structure to support the work in upgrades
- Examination of the schedule to find time to work on upgrades
- Expansion of the short-term implementation plan to include differentiated professional development opportunities to meet the varied needs of the teachers

The following field example underscores the importance of the two strands in this phase of the model.

Field Example

A suburban school on the West Coast had been working on implementing the Common Core State Standards into its local school curriculum. Our team trained the staff in unpacking the CCSS and translating them into language teachers could incorporate into their units. Because several different curricular areas were involved, our training focused on the Common Core Reading Standards for Informational Text and Writing and modeled how to integrate them in all curricular areas. After completing the unpacking and translating process, we transitioned to unit map design to show the teachers how they could integrate not only the unpacked and translated standards but also the digital upgrades.

We coached them through the elements in the unit: big ideas, essential questions, content, skills, assessments, activities, and resources. As we did, we shared specific examples of possible digital upgrades. One application was Popplet (http://popplet.com), which can be used to brainstorm ideas and organize them in a sequential manner. Another application great for organizing and presenting ideas is Blendspace (www.blendspace.com; formerly Edcanvas). This helped the teachers see the natural connections between the work they had been doing on the new standards using the MTTC process and the integration of the upgrades. In addition, the MTTC process provided the opportunity to coach for quality, as teachers mentally unpacked the content and skills that students would need to be successful at performing the upgrades. As they did this, teachers were able to crosscheck the alignment with elements in the unit that helped ensure a high-quality, tightly aligned unit.

Once the teachers had started the process of integrating the new literacies into their classroom units, they conducted a read-through to share their upgraded units with their colleagues and discuss the progression of projects, skills, and content. They then made adjustments to eliminate any gaps and repetitions.

Phase III: Integrating and Sustaining the Process

This phase focuses on the examination of data to inform the process. By using student work and assessment data, schools can adjust the training and process to strengthen the alignment with the curriculum and instruction in the classroom. The targets identified under support structure focus on expansion of communication and use of data.

Professional Development Content

Content and actions targeted in this phase include:

- Development of a schoolwide map of the new literacies across the curriculum

- Integration to 21st century strategies and skills

- Examination of student work and assessment data to inform unit upgrades and classroom instruction

Support Structure

The following represents a list of content that should be included in the professional development as schools transition to the Launching the Process phase:

- Development of a long-term implementation plan
- Development of a monitoring plan to determine adjustments needed to strengthen the process
- Development of a hub to support the professional development plan and promote the communication of materials and resources throughout the system

The following field example underscores the importance of the two strands in this phase of the model.

Field Example

We believe that it is important for all leaders and facilitators to develop their own webpages to share information with the educators they work with. Jacobs and Johnson (2012) describe a school webpage as a "hub" that allows for a direct connection to all members of the school community. The hub serves as a support resource enabling teachers and stakeholders to collaborate in the learning process. It also provides easy access to training materials, resources, and web 2.0 tools.

Through Bill's coaching, Ann began building her own professional development hub using Yola. This was empowering, because she could easily manage all of her professional development materials, web 2.0 tools, and design templates in one place for easy access during her work with schools implementing MTTC and integrating the new literacies. Ann loves the ease with which she can quickly share new materials or examples, and using a hub has transitioned her from the paper mode to modeling the use of digital application upgrades for leadership teams and teachers in a workshop setting. She has since developed her own in Wix.

Bill uses WordPress to maintain connections with educators whom he works with around North America. Through his blog, Bill posts one or two resources per month related to instructional technology and curriculum development, and he provides additional resources beyond what is shared in his workshops. WordPress provides the framework for teachers and administrators to create their own blogs and share new information within their own learning communities.

WordPress and Yola are only two of the many sites that school and leadership teams can use to manage documents and materials while providing enhanced communication opportunities with all stakeholders. We have worked with schools that have set up hubs on Google sites to house critical documents and materials and to foster ongoing communication. You could also consider building your own local school learning teams with Edmodo (www.edmodo.com), a social network that school leaders can use to facilitate conversations, distribute files, and conduct virtual meetings. A hub can be a tremendous asset to leadership teams in helping them manage aspects of the implementation process as well as opening the channels of communication with all stakeholders.

Phase IV: Advancing the Work

This phase addresses changes and the future. How does a school stay current? How can a school continually factor new innovations, discoveries, materials, and standards into their curriculum? In order to do so, the school must have processes and protocols in place that embrace change and encourage continual upgrades in the process. Phase IV targets change and focuses on continual renewal and upgrades.

Professional Development Content

The following content should be included in the professional development as schools transition to the Advancing the Work phase:

- Alignment with the new CCSS standards

- Examination of new literacies

- Replacement of dated content, skills, and assessment with new literacies

Support Structure

Targeting the following content will help ensure a strong infrastructure for lasting change when schools are working on Advancing the Work:

- Development of a protocol and process to stay current in new literacies

- Development of a site to house and organize critical applications

- Expansion of the leadership team to enhance training and leadership opportunities

- Expanded policies to support new literacies

The field example underscores the importance of the two strands in this phase of the model.

Field Example

A school in central Florida that has been very progressive in the integration of new literacies formed a Curriculum21 team to develop a process to share new sites and applications with colleagues. The team adapted its hub to include links and updates to help support this work. It also scheduled briefing updates via web and Skype sessions to share new tools and applications. During faculty meetings, the team included "upgrade moments" on the agenda, during which one person shared a new upgrade or resource. Periodically, the team met virtually instead of in person. While this was only a first step in developing procedures and protocols to address ongoing changes that impact curricular decisions, it provided the starting point on which to build.

We believe the implementation model we have just outlined provides the keystone for systemic implementation of the new literacies. By using it, leadership teams can avoid the pitfall of one-shot experiences. It also provides the framework through which professional learning can take place in an organized and thoughtful manner. We have found in our work that schools experience the most success when they develop a comprehensive plan that includes a focus on the initiative, the new literacies, and the support structure. This model helps to ensure a laser-like focus that is critical in supporting a school's commitment to providing 21st century learning opportunities for students.

Implementation Activities and Strategies

In this section, we suggest a sampling of specific activities and strategies that we have used with leadership teams as they targeted systemwide implementation using the new literacies implementation model. These activities and strategies suggest the types of mental and physical exercises a team could use as they work through the areas of focus in each phase of the model. To show the reader where the activity or strategy could be used in the model, we have also indicated the specific phase to which it aligns.

Identifying Your Leadership Team

Determining your leadership team is a critical first step and helps a leader to clarify his or her own role, as well as to think through the leadership team structure needed to sustain the work over the long term.

A leader should consider administrators, supervisors, and teacher leaders for the leadership team. In Santa Clara County, Melissa Christie's team included about fifteen people who were curriculum coordinators or provided tech support. Each represented a faction of the population and brought perspectives and insights that proved invaluable in formulating a well-designed plan.

In another school, the leadership team was comprised of the curriculum coordinator, each building principal, two teacher leaders from each elementary school, six teacher leaders from the middle school, and eight teacher leaders from the high school. This support structure worked well, but as the school continued to work on its vision and plan, the team leaders found it beneficial to add the special education supervisor and technology director, too.

In both schools, once the school leader had identified the leadership team, the team members drafted a purpose statement. They then brainstormed where they would be in three years if they implemented the new literacies. They considered the products and processes that would be produced or developed. Then, they considered what they would see happening in the classroom and what would be different as a result of implementing the new literacies. Through this exercise, they began to create a shared vision.

The teams next worked to clarify their own roles and responsibilities. They used a three-column grid. In the first column, they identified the various people on their team—the curriculum coordinator, principals, teacher leaders, technology specialist, special education supervisors, and so on. In the second column, across from each name, they identified the specific roles and responsibilities of each person. In the third column, they added the training needed for team members to be successful in their role. Having determined their purpose, drafted a shared vision, and identified their roles and responsibilities, they were ready to proceed with developing their goals and implementation plan.

Connecting the Work on New Literacies With Other Initiatives

Another critical step for a leadership team in the early stages of implementation is to make connections with other school improvement initiatives. Many schools are working on multiple school improvement initiatives at once. As a result, there is a tendency for staff to view them all as disconnected events, and this causes stress and anxiety as they work to balance everything. We encountered this in a workshop on the East Coast. During the overview of the new literacies, we heard teachers express both excitement and nervousness. One teacher said, "I would love to do this, but what do I give up so I have time to do it?" It was apparent by the reaction of those around her that others in the group shared this sentiment.

We used this as an opportunity to connect the dots. We asked each table team of eight teachers to brainstorm what they felt the added value was for students as a result of implementing the new literacies into their units. Next, we asked teachers to brainstorm other initiatives they were working on and had started implementing over the past few years. After they had identified the initiatives, we asked them to divide the list of initiatives so pairs of people had two or three to discuss. We then asked each pair to identify the added value for students of each initiative and discuss possible connections to the new literacies: "What was the fit?" The teachers then shared their findings with the rest of the team.

This activity helped teachers understand how the integration of new literacies could take their work to the next level. Teams could use a number of digital applications to support this activity, such as the following:

- **Inspiration** (www.inspiration.com)
- **Bubbl.us** (https://bubbl.us)
- **Padlet** (http://padlet.com)

Setting Realistic Goals

As we work with leadership teams in the goal-setting process, we often find that their initial goals tend to be general in nature, as in the following typical responses.

- "We want staff members to deepen their understanding of the new literacies."
- "We want each staff member to implement the new literacies into his or her curriculum."
- "We want staff members to use the new literacies to upgrade their curriculum."

While these goals are well intentioned, they are too general or lofty to be measurable. Goals need to be specific and measurable to be meaningful. We also believe that a goal should include evidence of success. By crafting goals in such a manner, leadership teams can use them to determine specific training the staff needs to successfully complete the goal.

Taking the goals listed here and using the goal-setting coaching points, a refined goal for the first semester might be:

> Teachers will target one unit they currently teach and edit it to include a specific new literacy. The unit will also include any additional content and skills students will need to be successful. After implementing the unit, teachers will share sample student work at

a professional development session and discuss the value added
to the unit.

We begin by modeling a similar goal for the team. We then ask team members
to target one of their goals that they feel is general and brainstorm the specific
steps needed to successfully meet it, including evidence showing it had been met.
What products would be produced during the training? By using these steps, a
leadership team can edit its goals so they are clearly stated, specific, and measurable. When teams break a goal down into specific steps, they have not only a
shared understanding of the expectations but also a better estimate of the amount
of time they need for training.

Differentiating Professional Development

Sometimes less is more when it comes to professional development days. We
find this is particularly true when working with the new literacies. Teachers need
a chance to digest them, see concrete examples, and consider how the examples
apply to them.

It often helps to set the stage with onsite training, particularly when doing an
overview. During the overview, a leadership team is laying the foundation with
the goal of getting everyone on the same page from the beginning. However, just
as in a classroom, you will find that some teachers are ready to move forward
quickly while others need more examples and a chance to work with colleagues to
consider a specific application in their classroom. The most effective professional
development is tailored to meet the staff's needs. Consider some of the following
possibilities:

- Targeted web sessions on each new literacy, during which the facilitator
  models how to get started

- Targeted web sessions focused on specific applications in units

- Targeted coaching sessions with specific strategies to help teachers
  sharpen the alignment among the elements in a unit

- Minisessions that focus on specific training needs

- Small-group sessions for those who may be less tech savvy

- Short professional development sessions for modeling examples

- Informal targeted coaching sessions with two or three teachers to
  address specific aspects of the training that they may be confused about
  or struggling with

Developing an Implementation Map

We have found that mapping an implementation plan is an effective way for a team to organize its training. It breathes life into the shared vision and serves as a tremendous communication tool for all stakeholders. Schools we have worked with that have taken the time to develop a comprehensive implementation plan are focused and far more productive in meeting their goals.

We coach teams to think about each training session as they would a unit. Their professional development unit would include coaching in the following areas:

- Date and time frame of the training

- Areas of focus for the session identified in a goal-setting activity

- The big idea of the training that answers the question, Why are we doing this?

- Essential questions to engage staff and focus the training

- Content that facilitators need to teach during the training

- Skills that participants should be able to demonstrate as a result of the training

- Implementation activities they plan to use to engage the staff

- Products or evidence of success the teams produce during the session

- Materials or resources the team needs for the training

- Assignment for the next session

We encourage readers to refer to the sample professional development map of a few sessions (table 3.2, page 80). In addition, *The Curriculum Mapping Planner: Templates, Tools, and Resources for Effective Professional Development* (Jacobs & Johnson, 2009) and the LiveBook and LivePlanner from *Mapping to the Core: Integrating the Common Core State Standards Into Your Local School Curriculum* (Jacobs, 2012) detail this process of developing an implementation plan. We have adapted the process covered in these texts for the new literacies.

Some schools don't include all the components on their implementation maps in the beginning, but as they become more skilled and confident, they add the others. Additionally, teams can easily expand the sample plan into a yearlong plan that incorporates multiple goals. Leaders and leadership teams have found implementation maps extremely helpful in laying out a comprehensive implementation plan. Many teams share the plan with staff, boards of education, parents, and other stakeholders. Using an electronic format for the maps, teams can

Table 3.2: Professional Development Plan for Integrating ActivInspire Into the Curriculum

Dates	Session 1 6 Hours	Session 2 6 Hours	Follow-Up Web Session 1 Hour
Areas of Focus	• ActivInspire as an upgrade • Implications for instruction • Sample ActivInspire activities	• Alignment with standards and units • Step-by-step process to integrate ActivInspire into the curriculum	• Review process • Coaching strategies to ensure quality implementation
Essential Questions	• How can the ActivInspire activities upgrade instructional units? • How can students engage in authentic 21st Century experiences of learning using ActivInspire and a Promethean Board?	• How can ActivInspire activities integrate the state standards, Common Core standards and career readiness standards into the curriculum? • What design strategies can be used to ensure quality implementation and alignment with the curriculum?	• How can the mapping review process be used as a tool to upgrade our maps? • What coaching strategies can be used to ensure high-quality use of ActivInspire?
Content	• Definition of upgrades: Upgrading and replacing traditional content, and traditional content delivery, with ActivInspire and a Promethean Board • Rationale and purpose of the integration of the ActivInspire system into the classrooms • Sample ActivInspire activities that include nonnegotiables—big ideas, essential questions, content, and skills that are essential in all ActivInspire activities • Alignment with 21st century skills • Benefits and value added	• Design strategies that we can use to integrate digital 2.0 applications in our curriculum. • Step-by-step process to develop authentic ActivInspire activities that reflect the nonnegotiables • ActivInspire activity design strategies, Promethean Planet resources, on-demand media, and web 2.0 tools integrated into ActivInspire activities in all curricular areas	• ActivInspire review process • Benefits of the review process • Purpose of the review process • Coaching strategies to ensure quality units

Continued →

Dates	Session 1 6 Hours	Session 2 6 Hours	Follow-Up Web Session 1 Hour
Skills and Steps in the Process	• Identify a unit to upgrade where you could integrate ActivInspire activities. • Brainstorm possible ActivInspire activities you could integrate into your curriculum. • Identify additional skills that align with the ActivInspire activities. • Include the basic skills in ActivInspire Flip Chart development using the Promethean ActivInspire rubric. • Explain how ActivInspire could be used to integrate 21st century skills and upgrade the curriculum. • Discuss the potential benefits to students.	• Use the process to develop an ActivInspire activity to integrate into your unit. • Replace or delete dated content. • Determine precise ActivInspire skills and level of understanding of how to use ActivInspire tools. • Align ActivInspire content and skills to standards. • Use standards to cross-check for alignment of the ActivInspire activities. • Integrate 21st century skills using ActivInspire resources. • Use advanced ActivInspire strategies to refine maps.	• Review ActivInspire activities across the grades to determine progression and address repetitions. • Apply strategies to edit your own ActivInspire activities. • Continue to work on additional content area ActivInspire lessons. • Develop a timeline and determine next steps. • Identify the benefits of the review process.
Evidence or Artifacts	• ActivInspire activities that reflect upgraded content and 21st century skills • Live teacher demonstrations of ActivInspire activities	• Create a web-based HUB for generated ActivInspire activities. • Produce a video of a student project presented with ActivInspire and the Promethean Board.	• Share upgraded lessons. • Update the web-based HUB for generated lessons.

Continued →

Dates	Session 1 6 Hours	Session 2 6 Hours	Follow-Up Web Session 1 Hour
Assignment	• Jacobs, H. H. (2010). *Curriculum 21: Essential Education for a Changing World*. Alexandria, VA:; Association for Supervision and Curriculum Development. (Chapters 1–3 & 12) • Promethean Planet ActivInspire Training Guide, www.prometheanplanet.com/en-us /professional-development/getting-started /get-started-with-the-activclassroom • Chapter 1 in Martin-Kniep, G. (2000), *Becoming a Better Teacher*. Alexandria, VA: Association for Supervision and Curriculum Development, and chapter 5 in McTighe, J., and Wiggins, G. (2005), *Understanding by Design*. Alexandria, VA: Association for Supervision and Curriculum Development	• Jacobs, H. H. *Mapping to the Core: Integrating the Common Core Standards into Your Local School Curriculum*. Salt Lake City: School Improvement Network Publications • Curriculum 21 Clearinghouse: http:// curriculum21.com/clearinghouse • Georgia, Common Core, and National Curriculum Standards: http:// livebinders.com/play/play/70725	• Promethean Planet Professional Development Resources: • http://prometheanplanet .com

continuously edit and adjust them as necessary, just as teachers adapt lesson plans in a classroom. Training sessions need not dictate the progress teams can make when planning for implementation.

Monitoring the Plan

Is the integration of the new literacies positively impacting student achievement? What additional professional development might we need to take upgrades to the next level? By taking the time to construct clearly stated goals and a well-crafted comprehensive implementation plan, leadership teams can use monitoring tools and protocols to collect the specific feedback teams need to revise the plan to ensure high-quality work and determine the impact on student achievement. Teams can then use the data to make adjustments in the process to maximize the impact.

Teams can use a number of digital applications to collect feedback. InfuseLearning (www.infuselearning.com) is an effective tool to collect data from your faculty. You can quickly set up questions about upcoming professional development and send them out electronically. Another website that teams often use is Survey Monkey (www.surveymonkey.com).

One school developed survey questions in Poll Everywhere that aligned to the detailed steps identified in their goals. Following each training, the leadership team had the staff complete the survey, and the team used the data from the survey to adjust the training as it went along.

Another school aligned survey questions to the detailed steps identified in their goals. Following each training, the leadership team asked the staff to complete the survey and used the data from the survey to adjust the training as it went along.

A third school built a feedback loop into its implementation process. Once every six weeks, the team asked teachers to target a unit in which they had integrated new literacies and to bring sample student work and assessment data. They also developed a protocol that the data teams could use to determine the impact of the integration on student achievement. This school specifically targeted 21st century skills, higher-order thinking, and technology skills. Through this process, they were able to edit their units so they had a greater impact on learning.

Conclusion

In this chapter, we have shared some very practical examples and strategies to help schools get started in the process of implementing the new literacies into their curriculum. As you embark on this journey, the key points in the following sections regarding technology and implementation can serve as a checklist to help you lay an infrastructure for long-term success.

Key Points: Technical

The following list can guide you with technical issues:

- Adequate wireless infrastructure is critical. Applications in this chapter require an Internet connection.

- Desktop computers, laptops, tablets, and other mobile devices must be secure.

- Internet-use policies should be up to date and prominently displayed in all classrooms and labs.

- The school should implement a BYOD or bring-your-own-technology (BYOT) plan to take advantage of teacher- and student-owned mobile devices.

- The school should upgrade technology policies to allow students to use cell phones as learning tools.

- The IT department should conduct technology hardware audits and inventories annually.

- Schools should have procedures in place for volume purchases of mobile device applications.

Key Points: Implementation

The following list can guide you during implementation:

- Form your leadership team and clarify its purpose, roles, and responsibilities.

- Develop a shared vision.

- Take time to lay a foundation with staff so they have a deep understanding of the *whats* and *whys*.

- Make connections with other initiatives.

- Set specific realistic goals.

- Differentiate your professional development to meet the needs of your learners.

- Map a comprehensive implementation plan.

- Use feedback to monitor and adjust the plan.

- Train leaders and teachers in using the new literacies to upgrade their meetings, classroom units, and instruction.

When integrating the new literacies into the curriculum, leadership is the non-negotiable. Teachers need examples, models, and resources to successfully integrate the new literacies into their curricula. They also need the new literacies broken down into practical terms and doable steps so they can experience success. This creates the excitement and energy to go further into the process.

References and Resources

Advanced Learning Technologies project at the University of Kansas Center for Research on Learning (ALTEC). (2012). *Assign-A-day.* Accessed at http://assignaday.4teachers.org on October 1, 2012.

Apple. (2012a). *Apple in education: iTunes U.* Accessed at www.apple.com/education/itunes-u on October 1, 2012.

Apple. (2012b). *Find out how: Enjoying and organizing your video.* Accessed at www.apple.com/findouthow/movies/ on October 1, 2012.

Alcock, M., Jacobs, H. H., Johnson, A., & Sullivan, D. (2012). *Mapping your Common Core implementation plan: A step-by-step process.* Midvale, UT: School Improvement Network.

The Archive. (2012). *Understanding 9/11: A television news archive.* Accessed at https://archive.org/details/911 on October 1, 2012.

Creativity Portal. (2012). *Creativity portal: Transforming through creativity, consciousness, and kindness.* Accessed at www.creativity-portal.com/prompts/imagination.prompt.html on October 1, 2012.

Curriculum Designers Inc. (2012a). *Curriculum 21 clearinghouse.* Accessed at www.curriculum21.com/clearinghouse on September 15, 2012.

Curriculum Designers Inc. (2012b). *Curriculum 21 global partnership.* Accessed at www.c21hub.com/globalpartnership on October 1, 2012.

Education Northwest. (2012). *6+1 traits: Writing prompts.* Accessed at http://educationnorthwest.org/resource/514 on October 1, 2012.

Eduscapes. (2012). *Cool classroom pages.* Accessed at http://eduscapes.com/tap/topic60.htm on October 1, 2012.

Google Calendar. (2012). *Google Apps Learning Center.* Accessed at http://learn.googleapps.com/calendar on October 1, 2012.

Jacobs, H. H., & Johnson, A. (2012). *Mapping to the Core: Integrating the Common Core State standards into your local school curriculum.* Midvale, UT: School Improvement Network.

Jacobs, H. H., & Johnson, A. (2009). *The curriculum mapping planner: Templates, tools, and resources for effective professional development.* Alexandria, VA: Association for Supervision and Curriculum Development.

Library of Congress. (2012). *Teacher resources.* Accessed at www.loc.gov/teachers on October 1, 2012.

Microsoft. (2012). *Getting started with Windows Movie Maker.* Accessed at http://windows.microsoft.com/en-US/windows-vista/Getting-started-with-Windows-Movie-Maker on October 1, 2012.

Miller, S. (2012). *50 ways to use Twitter in the classroom.* Accessed at www.teachhub.com/50-ways-use-twitter-classroom on October 1, 2012.

Madeleine Maceda Heide, EdM, is currently the director at Academia Cotopaxi in Quito, Ecuador. Prior to that, she was assistant superintendent for the American School of Bombay and before that principal at the Hong Kong International School, principal at the International School of Brussels, and a teacher at Taipei American School. Madeleine has done extensive teacher training, presentations, consulting work, and university-level teaching in the Philippines, Taiwan, Belgium, the Netherlands, Hong Kong, China, Chile, India, and the United States. She has always been passionate about supporting the growth and development of adult educators. A career of working closely with many talented teachers, parents, students, and administrators around the world has increased her enthusiasm for innovative teaching and learning practices and the school structures that support them. To learn more about Madeleine's work, follow her on Twitter @MadeleineHeide.

Fiona Reynolds, EdM, is the director of teaching and learning at the American School of Bombay. Prior to this, she was an administrator in both the American School of Bombay and Graded School in Sao Paulo and has been an international educator for seventeen years, working in Brazil, India, the Ivory Coast, Mexico, and Poland. Her current focus is leveraging the expertise of the teachers in her school to develop small- and large-scale professional learning communities. Fiona has presented at a variety of conferences on superstructing schools, organizing schools for change, creating developmentally appropriate middle schools, and setting a vision for young adolescent education. She has also consulted with a number of nongovernmental organizations to develop teacher-training programs and structures that support the learners these organizations serve.

To learn more about Fiona's work, follow her on Twitter @fionacrossthec.

Jane McGee, MA, is the high school principal and assistant superintendant at the American School of Bombay. Jane has worked in international education since 1993 in Italy, Egypt, Thailand, and Poland as a mathematics teacher, counselor, international baccalaureate coordinator, and principal. During this time, she has presented at numerous conferences on topics ranging from enhancing student learning through the integration of technology to implementing creative uses of distance learning.

Shabbi Luthra, PhD, is the director of research and development and technology at the American School of Bombay and works with a team of educators to develop new designs for schooling, teaching, and learning. She has worked for over two decades in international schools in the field of educational technology. Her work focuses on the development of stakeholder ownership of technology integration and on the creation of technology-enriched learning environments. Shabbi's blog, *Paradigm Shift* (http://paradigmshift21 .edublogs.org), shares reflections on schools and teaching and learning in the 21st century.

For more information about Shabbi's work, follow her on Twitter @shluthra.

Nitasha Chaudhuri, EdM, is an associate principal at the American School of Bombay and has been an international educator since 2000. Additionally, she oversees the development of the school's Early Childhood Education Center program. She has experience in teaching and working with early elementary children, an age group she is passionate about, in India and the United Kingdom and in training educators and students on 21st century skills.

For more information about Nitasha's work, follow her on Twitter @nitashac.

To learn more about the American School of Bombay, visit www.asbtal.weebly .com. To book Madeleine Maceda Heide, Fiona Reynolds, Jane McGee, Shabbi Luthra, or Nitasha Chaudhuri for professional development, contact pd@solution -tree.com.

Chapter 4

Getting to Superstruct: Continual Transformation of the American School of Bombay

By Madeleine Maceda Heide, Fiona Reynolds, Jane McGee, Shabbi Luthra, and Nitasha Chaudhuri

In the two-thousand-year-old city of Mumbai, India, the American School of Bombay (ASB) is thriving as a global innovator in education for the future. In its short, thirty-plus-year history, this school established an international reputation by staying on the cutting edge of best practices to ensure that its technology tools truly support and enhance teaching and learning. With its biennial conference, ASB Un-Plugged; an ASB Online Academy; multiple partnerships with leading companies, including TED, Google, and NuVuStudio; and a variety of public presentations at a number of international conferences, the American School of Bombay continues to flourish. The work of the faculty at ASB to support teacher growth and leadership in Mumbai through the Teacher Training Program, a two-year professional development program developed and run by ASB teachers, also speaks to the commitment of everyone at the school to the mission of enhancing the lives of others.

Mumbai lies on the west coast of India, with a deep natural harbor making it a major seaport. It is the capital city of the state of Maharashtra, the most populous city in India, and the fourth most populous city in the world. It is also the country's financial, commercial, and entertainment capital. In this bustling and vibrant city, life moves fast, and change is expected. Mumbaikars continually have to adjust to changes in their lives, whether dealing with traffic, religious celebrations in the streets, emerging wealth, or shifting political power. Perhaps this tolerance toward change has provided the American School of Bombay with an advantage, fostering its emergence as a premier school in terms of innovation.

This chapter will tell the story of how this extraordinary school began a journey and continues to transform itself beyond the basic integration of technology into a culture of innovation in all aspects. This chapter will chronicle three periods of time spanning from 2000 to 2012 and explain the key steps, decisions, and turning points in that journey. We hope our story will inspire others who are keen to transform their schools into teaching and learning environments in which innovation, creativity, critical thinking, and collaboration abound.

From Variable to Strategic: 2000–2008

In studying successful organizations, it is helpful to examine decisions or practices that started out one way and developed into something else. In our case, we are aware that some practices started out as variable (meaning they were accidental or fluctuating practices that relatively few people carried out) and our organization moved to becoming more strategic (that is, having intentional or deliberate practices as expectations or standards). We used these critical decisions and practices as a blueprint for future development.

In 2000, the American School of Bombay adopted a one-to-one laptop approach, with a commitment to "anytime, anywhere learning." This was a major strategic decision. ASB was one of the first international schools to commit to this approach. The school provided one laptop computer for each student in grades 6–12 to use daily in school and at home, laptops for elementary students to use during the school day, and laptops for every teacher. To assist teachers in learning how best to use technology within their diverse classrooms, the school created a technology department; a director of technology; technology coordinators for the elementary, middle, and high schools; and a team of technology support staff.

As with any new initiative, technology integration took time to gain ground. In those early years, some teachers enthusiastically embraced technology but many classrooms remained more conventional. The school leaders wanted technology integration to become more widespread, and so in 2006, they began an intentional campaign to build a new vision for the school and engage the community in a variety of ways. A strategic planning committee made up of faculty, parents, and students created the path to the new vision. The leaders crafted a new mission, as well as core values, strategic objectives, and strategies. These statements refocused ASB and positioned it for continuous improvement. The new mission statement was unique, highlighting attributes other than academic excellence and articulating values that the community held dear: "We inspire all of our students to continuous inquiry, empowering them with the skills, courage, optimism, and integrity to pursue their dreams and enhance the lives of others" (American School of Bombay, 2006). This mission statement was to serve the school for many years to come. It helped differentiate the school from others in Mumbai and boldly positioned it in the international community. The concepts of inspiring all, pursuing dreams, and enhancing lives are ones that people connect with and remember.

The Strategic Planning Committee agreed on five key objectives to establish systems and structures to support the school's development: (1) personnel, (2) subsystems, (3) curriculum, (4) facilities, and (5) commitment. The committee then created teams made up of representatives from different stakeholder groups. Discussions in each team produced a number of end results for every strategic objective, which would target the next phase of school improvement and act essentially as bridges between where the school was at the time and where it desired to be in the future. The director of technology created an end result specifically targeting technology: educational technology at ASB enriches student learning.

The director of technology also worked closely with other members of the leadership team to determine how best to accomplish this throughout the school and formed a technology leadership team (TLT). The TLT was composed of a group of twenty to thirty teachers, depending on the year, who helped to prototype new educational technologies in their classrooms. By having teachers become involved in this process, the change from a traditional classroom model to a one-to-one model became less a top-down decision and more of a community one. Teachers who were not comfortable with the use of technology went to colleagues on the TLT for help or coaching. The director of technology also worked proactively with the board of trustees and parents to understand the role of technology in education. In doing so, she was able to confront fears about the prolific use of technology in school, both among the faculty and the parent community. Her efforts consolidated the school's decision to adopt a one-to-one laptop approach and put to rest any concerns about technology.

The Technology Leadership Team

The technology leadership team strategized and facilitated technology use throughout the school and addressed the technology end results. These were finding and developing educational technology tools, building technology integration to support learning, and developing a technological system that was robust enough to support the one-to-one laptop usage. This team was composed of a cross-section of the community, including teachers from elementary, middle, and high school; staff representatives; parents; and high school students. Having teachers, parents, and students on this team served a distinctive purpose. Parents were deeply interested in the quality of their children's education and convinced of the value of a premium education. Students were digital natives and critical consumers of technology tools and were powerfully invested in decision making around technology. As direct users, teachers had a forum for discussing the appropriate uses of technology in their own classrooms. Having a mixed group of teachers, staff, parents, and students proactively involved in building the school's technology integration program was empowering to all those involved. These individuals were highly engaged and invested in the successful integration of technology, thus forming an environment in which collaboration and innovation became widespread. The technology leadership team developed a vision statement and a set of belief statements that formed the basis for a technology integration plan (see figure 4.1). They developed responsible-use policies and a digital citizenship program. They also examined the International Society for Technology in Education (ISTE) teacher technology standards and developed a program of professional development to support teachers in integrating technology based on the ISTE standards (ISTE, 2008).

The first international American School of Bombay conference took place in 2008 after two years of planning. ASB Un-Plugged (www.asbunplugged.org) was a response to requests from other schools that wished to start a similar one-to-one laptop program. Participants selected workshops relevant to their needs from strands in administration, instructional integration, and technology support. Scott McLeod, Stewart Crais, and David Quinn, all notable specialists in the fields of technology integration in education, gave keynote presentations. The students in the ASB technology crew were major stars, actively demonstrating their expertise in technology as well as their ownership of their own learning.

The conference showcased classrooms, teachers presented workshops, and students participated in presentations. The preparation for opening classrooms was a way for the teachers at ASB to reflect upon their work of integrating technology and to share their learning. Educators witnessed firsthand how ASB's students, staff, and community embraced innovation, change, and leadership in education for the 21st century. The conference set the pace for technology integration in international schools and positioned ASB as an innovative school for the digital age. Even more importantly, ASB became known as a school that openly shared its experiences with others and took an interest in guiding other schools as they developed new environments for digital learning.

AMERICAN SCHOOL OF BOMBAY TECHNOLOGY VISION STATEMENT AND BELIEF STATEMENTS 2008

We envision a world at ASB where purposeful, integrated uses of technology tools inspire creativity and innovation, support continuous inquiry, foster collaboration, enhance learning and achievement in all academic areas, and enable students to develop critical-thinking skills, apply information literacy, and manage complexity. We envision a world at ASB where all members of the community understand and model respectful, responsible, and ethical uses of technology in academic, social, and personal contexts.

The following belief statements continue to guide the realization of our vision.

- Teachers can be most effective when they facilitate collaborative student learning through a wide variety of media-rich, interactive, and authentic learning experiences.
- Students can thrive in an increasingly digital world when teachers and administrators effectively model lifelong learning and collaboration.
- Parents can play a major role in the education of their children when they work with teachers to connect formal and informal uses of technology.
- Stakeholders from every sector of a learning community can be empowered to become leaders and effect positive change.
- A responsible learning community is dedicated to modeling and facilitating a clear understanding of the social, ethical, and legal issues and responsibilities related to our evolving digital culture.

Figure 4.1: American School of Bombay 2008 technology vision and belief statements.

Source: American School of Bombay, 2008.

Evolution to a Focus on Student Learning: 2008–2011

Following the success of the first conference, requests poured into ASB from other schools, asking for advice, sharing ideas, inviting collaboration, and requesting permission to visit. The program was a model for other schools, both private and public, regarding the process of moving from a computer-lab-style educational environment to one in which technology was ubiquitous. Systems and processes, including professional development strategies to educate the community about technology integration and a commitment of resources, were being solidly put in place.

The strategic plan brought new attention to student learning, and the purpose of technology integration became clearer; it was not a goal in itself but a tool for increased student learning. Energy was needed in the area of curriculum development, and leaders created a strategic objective in that area: "Align, and if necessary, develop curricula throughout the school to achieve our mission and strategic objective" (American School of Bombay, 2006, pg. 71). The following eight end results under this objective specifically pointed to establishing the systems and processes that would empower the school to focus on student learning:

1. ASB has implemented a curriculum design and review process driven by the mission and strategic objectives, which aligns the curriculum.

2. ASB consistently follows an assessment policy.

3. ASB assesses and supports the needs of all students.

4. The ASB curriculum promotes social responsibility through the inclusion of meaningful service learning at all grade levels.

5. Educational technology at ASB enriches student learning.

6. We develop our student data systems so that we can effectively assess our progress on our strategic objectives and collaborate to improve teaching and learning.

7. Twenty-first century digital tools enhance student learning, critical thinking, collaboration, communication, and achievement in all academic areas.

8. Efficient use of digital tools supports communications and administrative functions at ASB.

Designating a Leader

In the fall of 2008, the school created the position of assistant superintendent for education to ensure that these end results remained a priority and that the school made progress in the curriculum objective. The commitment to add a designated leader in order to achieve these end results was a significant contributor to the school's success. As a key educational leader, the assistant superintendent built professional development plans and a collaborative, results-based environment to enable a focus on curriculum development, instruction, and assessment.

One of the first charges to the assistant superintendent was to increase the focus on learning across the school in conjunction with the leadership team, which included the elementary, middle, and high school principals; the director of technology; the director of special projects, the chief operations officer; and the superintendent himself. The goal was to develop a common understanding of the curriculum development process, including the adoption of standards, identification of knowledge and skills, and development of assessments and instructional strategies. The superintendent assigned the assistant superintendent to the instructional team, a committee of teachers and principals, to ensure the successful completion of the end results of the curriculum strategy from the strategic plan and to provide oversight on decisions about professional development funds.

Implementing Curriculum Review

The school established a curriculum review process to evaluate each academic subject every five years (table 4.1, page 96). In this process, a group of divisional representatives came together to examine the selected subject area standards, units, and resources to ensure alignment across the school.

Strengthening Assessments

As the focus on curriculum and student learning began in earnest, we soon learned that teachers needed guidance on how to write units with a focus on standards, using enduring understandings and essential questions to guide assessment work. We needed to clarify that standards, when used to guide and amplify instruction, would strengthen overall academic achievement. Curricular teams were set up in each division to have deeper conversations about what we wanted our students to know and be able to do across disciplines and grade levels and, more importantly, about how we could evolve what we currently had in place. These conversations led to the adoption of updated discipline-specific standards that best met the learning goals of our school and would also ultimately prepare our students for higher education, the workforce, and adult life. Throughout the next three years, teachers spent significant time building curriculum maps using Rubicons Atlas curriculum mapping software to document and house their units. This process included identifying critical knowledge and skills and developing assessments aligned with the standards following the Understanding by Design process and framework (Wiggins & McTighe, 2005). Technology remained a part of these conversations, and the ISTE technology standards for students became another factor in our examination of our curriculum and assessment processes.

Throughout this time, we also began to recognize that our curriculum development work needed to be anchored in current best practices in assessment, with a stronger focus on instructional practices that improved student learning. We formulated two strategic end results for assessment.

1. ASB consistently follows an assessment policy.

2. ASB assesses and supports the needs of all students.

Table 4.1: Five-Year Curriculum Review Cycle

	Year One (2006–2007)	Year Two (2007–2008)	Year Three (2008–2009)	Year Four (2009–2010)	Year Five (2010–2011)	Year Six (2011–2012)
Study year[1]	Language Arts	Social Studies	Math	PE		Language Arts
Plan year[2]		Language Arts	Social Studies	Math	PE	
Implement and review year[3]			Language Arts	Social Studies	Math	PE
Implement and review year[3]				Language Arts	Social Studies	Math
Implement and review year[3]					Language Arts	Social Studies

[1] Research current standards, methodologies, and best practices; identify and develop proposed improvements.

[2] Develop yearlong plan to prepare for curriculum and instructional changes; begin curriculum updates.

[3] Confirm development of common assessments and curriculum unit updates; use atlas tools to begin review of articulation improvements.

The school invited an assessment specialist, Damian Cooper, to work with teachers for a week to build their understanding. An assessment committee of elementary, middle, and high school teacher volunteers spent a significant amount of time studying the work of Dylan Wiliam, Tom Guskey, Rick Stiggins, and Ken O'Connor to develop a common understanding of current best practices on assessment, grading, and reporting, as well as the power of using formative assessment strategies in the classroom. The assessment committee wrote an assessment policy outlining a core philosophy and expectations for classroom practice.

Middle and High School

The middle and high school departments worked together to review unit assessments with their subject area standards in mind, and common assessments were added to curriculum maps. Fran Prolman, a consultant, was invited to spend a week assisting secondary subject-specific departments (social studies, science, and so on) in understanding the role of standards in planning for assessment. Moving away from grading practice assignments, taking away points for late work, and grading collaborative projects individually took time, and we devoted many faculty and subject area meetings to this. We have to review and renew our commitment to best practices in assessment every year with our new and returning faculty to ensure understanding in the middle and high school.

Elementary School

The elementary school needed a more common approach to assessing literacy learning across all grades. Our approach was to build a holistic system to address assessment that informed instruction, effective instructional strategies that met the needs of all learners, and efficient intervention methods to close the gaps among students. Teachers collectively studied the balanced literacy approach, doing book studies together and dialoging about core instructional elements of reading and writing workshops. The elementary school adopted a literacy assessment that provided for different ability levels, with instruction and resources corresponding specifically to what students needed to learn next. Consultants trained teachers in using the Fountas and Pinnell Benchmark Assessment System (2007) to assess literacy learning from kindergarten through grade 5. The Fountas and Pinnell system helps teachers assess what level each of their students is currently reading at, provides book choices that are at the child's current challenge level, and provides resources and suggestions for how to scaffold the child's learning to the next reading level. In addition, we chose the Observation Survey of Early Literacy Achievement to assess emergent readers and writers in kindergarten and grade 1 (Clay, 2006). These common assessments provided an anchor for our elementary school that allowed teachers to focus their attention on research-based instructional practices that were proven to be effective.

Formative Assessment Study

In addition to common assessments, we wanted teachers to use assessment as a formative tool to promote learning, rather than only as a summative tool to measure learning. We wanted to ensure students received frequent and meaningful feedback about where they were in their learning and what they needed to do to improve it. In order to help our teachers understand formative assessment, we asked each grade-level team and each department to study an element of formative assessment over a period of two months and to share what they learned during one of our professional development days. Teachers were eager to show their learning to their colleagues in fun and interesting ways. They used video clips, games, wikis, blogs, and Google Drive to capture their ideas and experiences. On another professional development day, we invited several teachers who were more advanced in their use of formative assessment to lead miniworkshops and asked teachers to choose the sessions they wanted to learn more about. Also, we encouraged teachers to observe one another's classroom practice, with a focus on the use of assessment for learning. This work was buoyed by a course on formative assessment being offered through Boston University that a cohort of twenty teachers at ASB were taking. In a unit on classroom assessment, a major assignment was for teachers to demonstrate, using a variety of digital tools, the uses of assessment for learning within their own classrooms. An example of this is a tool called 5,4,3,2,1, an interview process in which the teacher gives feedback to the student using a Google form. The teacher gave the student the following feedback in five minutes: four things he or she liked about the student's lab, three benchmarks the student excelled on, two quick fixes, and one major focus.

With all of this attention to assessment, it was clear that a growing number of teachers possessed a solid understanding of how to use formative assessments to enhance and direct learning within their classrooms.

Making Changes to Grading and Reporting

With more awareness among the faculty regarding what was considered appropriate assessment practice, it was time to consider changes to our grading and reporting practices. To this end, the middle and high school divisions came together in a joint task force to study grading and reporting. After studying Tom Guskey's (2009) and Damien Cooper's (2007) research on grading and reporting and looking at the International Baccalaureate Approaches to Learning (International Baccalaureate, 2013), they made a key decision to separate achievement grades from grades about behavior within the learning environment. They determined the most critical elements of behavior they wanted their students to portray and then agreed on indicators of success in portraying those elements. In other words, they created a rubric. The result of their work, Approaches to Learning (ATL), described expected behaviors, habits, or attributes that contribute to positive student learning in three areas and included a rubric for assessing each area (table 4.2). The task force shared various drafts of the descriptors and rubric with teachers, students, and parents to obtain feedback and create a final version. Middle and high school teachers began to use this rubric to regularly provide students with feedback about their behavior. Academic grades measured progress only toward subject-area standards.

Table 4.2: Approaches-to-Learning Rubric for Middle and High School

Manages Time, Resources, and Commitments Responsibly	Demonstrates Intellectual Curiosity, Initiative, and Perseverance	Contributes to a Positive Learning Environment and Collaborates Effectively With Others
Student is in class on time and prepared with all materials.	Student is a self-directed learner.	Student treats others with kindness and respect.
Student completes and submits work on time.	Student is attentive and focused on learning.	Student listens to and respects others' ideas.
Student demonstrates organizational skills and strategies that are appropriate and effective.	Student reflects on and monitors progress.	Student shows respect for the physical environment.
Student attends class regularly and takes responsibility for work missed.	Student implements changes based on constructive criticism.	Student collaborates well when working in a group.
Student takes good care of resources and tools.	Student utilizes effective problem-solving skills to overcome challenges.	Student cooperates with others, including offering help when appropriate.
Student communicates appropriately and follows through with commitments.	Student seeks assistance appropriately.	Student acts responsibly in meeting group obligations.
	Student asks relevant and meaningful questions.	

The leadership team decided to adopt the Measures of Academic Progress (MAP) as an external standardized online assessment of mathematics, reading, and language usage, developed by Northwest Evaluation Association (NWEA, 2013). MAP is administered twice a year for grades one through nine. In addition to assessing academic standards in reading, language usage, and mathematics, the assessment compares data between U.S. and international peer schools. It is an adaptive assessment, adjusting its questions individually to match the ability level of each student. In other words, it provides harder questions when the student answers correctly and easier questions when the student does not answer correctly, thus ending up with a more accurate score of a student's ability level. The NWEA also provides additional resources for teachers to set goals and differentiate instruction to match student needs based on specific data about their readiness. Teachers were trained in administering the test and comparing the data with other assessment information they had. Bringing in an external assessment met some resistance, but as use of standards to guide instruction became the norm, the MAP test, which is aligned to our standards, was increasingly seen as a valuable instrument for instruction instead of simply a measure of student learning.

Rethinking the Learning Environment

As we dug deeper into our curriculum and assessment work, conversations around 21st century learning environments began to emerge. We considered current research-based instructional practices, questioned traditional notions of alignment and standards-based curriculum development, and thought deeply about different models of professional development. Information about web 2.0 was plentiful, and we read as much as we could. In 2009 and every year afterward, we read *The 2009 Horizon Report: K–12 Edition* (Johnson, Levine, Smith, & Smythe, 2009), which presented research-based predictions of emerging technologies. Our understanding of how the world was changing became stronger. With every new piece of information, we considered the implications for schooling for the future.

We started out feeling pleased with our work on aligning our curriculum, instruction, and assessment, yet we were occasionally puzzled over the notion of alignment. While we believed that research-based instructional practices and assessments impacted learning, we also knew that teaching was highly personal and required individual passion and creativity. At one point, we expected all teachers to use the same software tool, but we began to realize that this expectation around specific technology tools and software was no longer appropriate. The one-shoe-fits-all approach, necessary at one point to align faculty and students, no longer modeled 21st century thinking. We needed to encourage teachers to be innovative, thoughtful, and selective about their choices of technology tools if we wanted to optimize student learning in a 21st century environment. We decided to add a technology integration section to our curriculum maps and asked individual departments and grade levels to identify those digital tools that were most suited to teaching and learning for specific standards and units. Teachers began to explore a range of tools that would both support teaching and assess learning. Online tools became an area of focus as web 2.0 developed, and teachers began to use wikis, Nings, Microsoft OneNote, and the school portal to share information and interact virtually with their students. Rather than *requiring* teachers to use common digital tools, we encouraged them to try them out, learn how they worked, share their experiences, and determine for themselves what worked best.

As we engaged in discussions about instructional practice, teachers began to question why we needed a separate section for technology integration in our

Rubicon Atlas curriculum maps template (see page 95). If we were truly integrating technology, teachers said, that should be documented in Stage 3: Learning Plan of the Understanding by Design template (Wiggins & McTighe, 2005). We adapted our template to honor our teachers' request and celebrated how far we'd come in technology integration. The third and final stage of unit development—instruction—was in full swing. We developed a wiki identifying technology skills as well as useful tools for students and teachers to plan professional development for both current and future faculty. It was also a way to check which skills students learned and when different tools were taught. Elementary students increasingly used software to create digital stories and to gather, analyze, and present reports, and perhaps most impressively, they learned how to use online databases and our library software, Destiny Follett, to research and find information.

Using e-Portfolio

Early into the 2009 academic year, a group of teachers in the elementary school began experimenting with e-Portfolio to replace paper student portfolios. As the teachers observed their students, they witnessed the role of technology in aiding metacognition. They began to reflect on the value of self-directed learning as the foundation for all learning. As their students began to take ownership of the process, the results were both amazing and humbling. These young students articulately explained how they were planning their project work, how they needed to collaborate with each other when they were stuck, and how they chose certain products not because they were their best work but because they showed what they were learning at the time. These teachers had created an environment in their classrooms in which students were able to reflect on their work over a period of time and think about how they could improve. Assessment *for* learning—the approach we took to achieve the strategic end result on the learning subpoint that required "ASB to consistently follow one assessment policy" (ASB, 2006, p. 60)—had been achieved. Our students had gained awareness of themselves as learners by using e-Portfolio, and our teachers felt empowered by their ownership of the process.

At the end of the school year, our head of school gave each staff member his or her summer reading—the book *Drive* (Pink, 2009). Reading that book was an important turning point in our collective learning. We began to talk in terms of 21st century skills and a school for the future. While the terms may have been somewhat simplistic, they captured the notion of a new and progressive approach to teaching and learning.

Expanding the Vision to the Community

As members of the leadership team continued to engage one another, this shift in our thinking, now through a 21st century skills lens, had widespread implications. If we were expecting our faculty and students to be flexible and adaptable in the use of technology, then shouldn't our board and parents be engaged as well? We decided to provide each member of the board of trustees with the use of a laptop computer for meetings and purchased a software program called BoardDocs. This was a commitment to paperless board meetings and a more efficient way to document and archive board documents. More importantly, this decision would require board members to become more adept in their own computer skills as they were placed squarely as learners within a 21st century learning environment. We were aligning ourselves with *Disrupting Class* (Christensen, Johnson, & Horn, 2008), a book about how schools must change to meet the needs of all students and prepare them for any number of possible futures. We supported our board members with training sessions, and they informed our thinking about providing technological support at an executive level. They became more aware of themselves as learners too, critically reflecting on their own learning. The vision of what it meant to be a 21st century learner was expanding.

We began to offer workshops and courses to help parents learn more about the range of digital tools utilized at the school. This deepened their understanding of our program, assisted them in their expectations for their children, and supported a strong school-home partnership. Our technology coordinators offered monthly tutorials, introducing parents to technology that their children were using in classrooms and inviting them to try out different tools. This became so popular that parents began to request more sessions. We eventually appointed a parent technology representative, who led weekly workshops to assist parents in bettering their skills. In addition, the parent technology representative began training other parent technology tutors. Soon, ASB's Online Academy was born and quickly became successful in offering technology courses for parents and, eventually, professional courses for teachers.

Forming New Partnerships

The breadth of our professional development began to shift and expand. We identified new sources of expertise and promoted internal resources as much as possible. We sought additional funding to provide for our increased appetite for professional growth. We sought partnerships with external organizations, collaborating and sharing our resources, but also as a means to further extend our learning and broaden our exposure to new ideas. As faculty members explored new technology tools and their implications for student learning, they were encouraged to share with their colleagues. Faculty were given time to present to colleagues during professional development day miniconferences and faculty meetings. Teachers were also encouraged to share their knowledge and skills at professional international conferences, and we received significant funding to cover a large portion of these costs. Our teachers were presenting at professional organizations such as the Near East South Asia Council of Overseas Schools, the European League for Middle Level Education, and the International Society for Technology in Education. We established a partnership with Boston University and offered a master's program to ASB faculty around 21st century skills, including technology integration and assessment practices. Outside consultants continued to offer professional development for division- and schoolwide initiatives, and another ASB Un-Plugged was in the making with a focus on technology integration in more evolved one-to-one school programs.

As technology integration became commonplace, we formalized pedagogical practices and raised our expectations. The tools individuals and small groups initially identified morphed into common expectations for all members of a grade level or discipline. The skill of effectively identifying and utilizing appropriate technological tools to support student learning was now part of being a successful teacher at ASB. We updated responsible-use policies and digital citizen documents to reflect the additional responsibility of faculty and students to support and maximize their own 21st century learning.

The Design Years: 2010–2012

Turnover in international schools is a given; it is a natural part of living internationally. Every year, about 25 percent of our students and about 15 percent of our faculty transition to new schools. In 2010, the American School of Bombay brought in a new head of school and a new elementary school principal. In 2011, a new middle school principal joined the leadership team. This turnover is also a feature of our board of trustees. By the fall of 2010, 50 percent of the board of trustees who had hired the new head of school had moved on to new posts, and new members began their term of office. Given the transient nature of our school, it was important that the systems, structures, operations, and processes were flexible and strong enough to survive various leadership transitions. With every transition, there was the risk of losing what we had gained, alongside the potential for new skills and energy. Keeping the balance was important.

A New Strategic Plan

In the fall of the 2010 school year, we launched a new strategic planning process, as it had been five years since our last one. We involved over seventy members of our community in a yearlong process in which we re-evaluated our school mission, core values, and strategic objectives. The result was an exciting new vision for the school, with specific areas for attention and new end results. We were building on the great work that had taken place and ensuring a robust future for our community. We reinstated our mission and all of our core values and added new ones to represent current areas of interest and need. Our new plan outlined four strategic objectives—learning, talent, advancement, and resources—each with specific end results to accomplish in the five-year period from 2011 to 2016.

Critical Role of Book Study

Reading professional material was already a shared value of our leadership team and one that we promoted among our faculty. Every year we gave teachers a book to read during the summer, and upon our return in August, this common focus sparked conversations and plans for the year. We continuously shared new books we were reading and exchanged them with one another. Our shared readings included *The Last Lecture* by Randy Pausch (2008); *The Tipping Point, Blink*, and *Outliers* by Malcolm Gladwell (2000, 2005, 2008); *Good to Great* by Jim Collins (2001); *Mindset* by Carol Dweck (2006); *The Fifth Discipline* by Peter Senge (1990); and *Immunity to Change* by Robert Kegan and Lisa Laskow Lahey (2009). We didn't necessarily engage in formal book studies or even regular conversations about these books. Instead, we were feeding our voracious appetites, seeking to expand our own ideas and knowledge and sharing what we learned on a more informal basis. We purchased some of these books in bulk for our committees and task forces, and soon large groups of teachers were reading the same books and engaging in discussions about the ideas. Professional reading was impacting our school culture.

As our teachers continued to grow and learn, the leadership team followed suit. In 2010, the team began to regularly have conversations around 21st century learning and what that should look like at ASB. To deepen this conversation, members spent a semester reading two books, *21st Century Skills: Rethinking How Students Learn* (Bellanca & Brandt, 2010) and *Curriculum 21: Essential Education for a Changing World* (Jacobs, 2010). We also read various blogs and articles about 21st century schools, notably the *21st Century School* series from

Independent School Management (2010). Each leadership team member presented significant ideas from specific readings each week, provoking thoughtful dialogue and visions of the ways in which they aligned with the mission and core values of our school.

We began to prioritize what was important to us as individuals, as a leadership team, and as members of the school community. These were not easy or simple conversations—there was much at stake, and we wrestled with each other's assumptions, priorities, and preferences. However, these difficult conversations were productive for us as a team, enabling our own professional growth and allowing dialogue and understanding to emerge. We began to understand some of the significant changes we would need to make in our systems, processes, and ways of approaching teaching and learning to become a school for the future. After significant research and dialogue, the team chose to adopt the enGauge model as a base and modified it to align with the needs of our particular school and community of learners (Burkhardt et al., 2003). The enGauge model identified four competencies that were important in the 21st century: digital-age literacy, inventive thinking, effective communication, and high productivity. Within these competencies, enGauge described a variety of more specific skills (Bellanca & Brandt, 2010).

Planning for the New Building

Another driver of change was also emerging; for years, our board had been exploring a variety of expansion options to accommodate the changing needs of our school. The board members' conversations were becoming more and more concrete, and the concept of a new school facility seemed more possible than ever before. The kind of learning we envisioned was just not possible in our existing facilities, which were very cramped. Teachers in the elementary school taught small groups in the hallway; physical education teachers were constantly asked to relocate their classes, since the gym was required for other events; our performing arts program had inadequate space to perform; many of our secondary teachers did their planning work in the library; meeting spaces were limited; high school students had no space of their own and often were crammed in with younger students. As we discussed our physical facility needs, we became increasingly excited about what might be possible if we were to have a brand-new facility. Ideas about 21st century learning environments were plentiful, and our community was buzzing.

Superstructing

At the end of the 2010–2011 school year, the strategic plan was completed. The reality of a new physical facility was growing closer, and we began reading about architecture, design, and space. After our intensive study of 21st century schools, the leadership team felt a sense of urgency about re-organizing and considering different systems and structures to obtain our goals. We were introduced to the work of Jane McGonigal, a game designer and author of the *New York Times* bestselling book *Reality Is Broken: Why Games Make Us Better and How They Can Change the World* (2011). Her game *Superstruct* was a massively multiplayer future-forecasting game that more than seven thousand people played from September to November 2008 (Kirchner, 2010). Her ideas on gaming and *superstructing* intrigued us. Superstructing is "reinventing our tools and processes, our organizational structures, and even our concepts of cooperation and collaboration" (McGonigal, 2009, pg. 1). McGonigal chose the idea of superstructing because it meant building on foundations that were already there, and we felt the same about ASB. We were building on the foundations laid by the initial strategic plan.

McGonigal's five indicators of reinvention necessary for success in an evolving field provoked us to rethink our structures and processes, even some that we had only begun using with the previous strategic plan. According to McGonigal (McGonigal, 2009), you know you're superstructing when:

1. You've achieved more and different participation
2. You begin to implement what once were nearly inconceivable possibilities
3. You're inventing and testing smaller and bigger practices
4. You are creating stranger and more shareable products
5. You are designing and participating in new and world-changing processes

Reading and talking about these ideas sparked our own thinking. We wanted to reinvent some of our structures and systems and reprioritize the skills we valued for our school. We scheduled a series of work sessions and retreats for our leadership team and started laying out which systems needed reinvention or rethinking. We also started drawing our ideas to help us figure out connections and relationships and make them clear to one another (figure 4.2). Later on, we began to see how visual thinking was a tool to innovate. We started using the metaphor of the moon as our dream goal. We created a visual ladder to the moon to share with our community: the rungs were structures, and the two bars on the side were our mission and core values, holding us together. The atmosphere

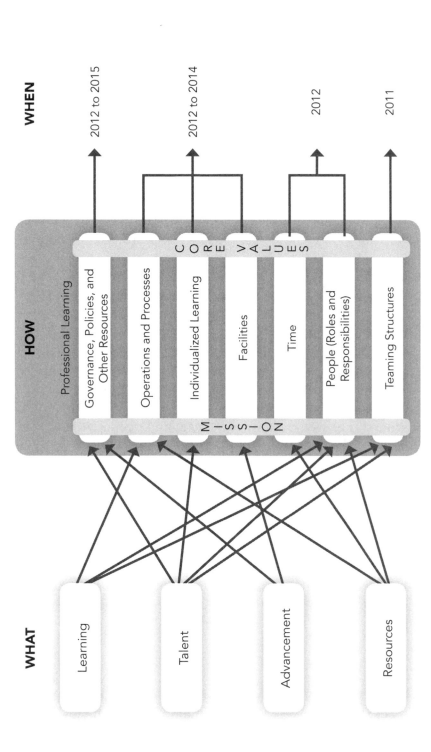

Figure 4.2: Superstructing for a 21st century school.
Source: Superstruct Presentation NESA Fall Leadership Conference, 2011.

around us was our professional learning environment. We came up with governance, policies, and other resources; operations; learning; facilities; time; people (roles and responsibilities); and team structures. We then tied each of these to a specific end result in our strategic plan and began writing work plans.

We found our attention drawn to the way we used time and the way we organized our faculty to do work. Armed with the provocative ideas from Jacobs, McGonigal, and Pink, we started asking ourselves a number of tough questions. Was there another way to get our work done more effectively and meaningfully? How might we think of autonomy, mastery, and purpose as drivers of our work rather than requirements and expectations? How could we try out new ideas or new tools within our classrooms without causing chaos or disruption to existing expectations? How might we leverage our faculty's skills and share leadership for our strategic plan? How could we begin using 21st century skills ourselves and pushing our own boundaries?

The Core Teams

Our ideas were evolving. We conceived two core teams as a basic element of our new structure. We established the Teaching and Learning (T&L) Core Team, whose purpose was to facilitate classroom teachers in implementing identified research-based best practices in the area of personalizing learning and 21st century skills. We also created the Research and Development (R&D) Core Team, whose purpose was to study, prototype, design, and develop new practices or tools in order to make recommendations for highly impactful practices for the future. We decided to abolish the requirement that all teachers participate and invited participation from anyone interested. We also decided that rather than mandate a common method for accomplishing the work, we would empower task force leaders to determine what, when, and how they would accomplish their objectives. When we rolled out this model (figure 4.3) to our faculty early in the 2011–2012 school year, the positive responses we received delighted us. Many teachers volunteered, and those who chose not to participate felt empowered to make their own decisions about how to focus their professional energies. Our new approach had begun.

The Teaching and Learning Core Team

In order to link our strategic plan end results with our superstruct work, we decided that the following two end results in the area of learning would be the focus of the T&L Core Team:

1. **Individualized learning**—ASB promotes a culture of high student

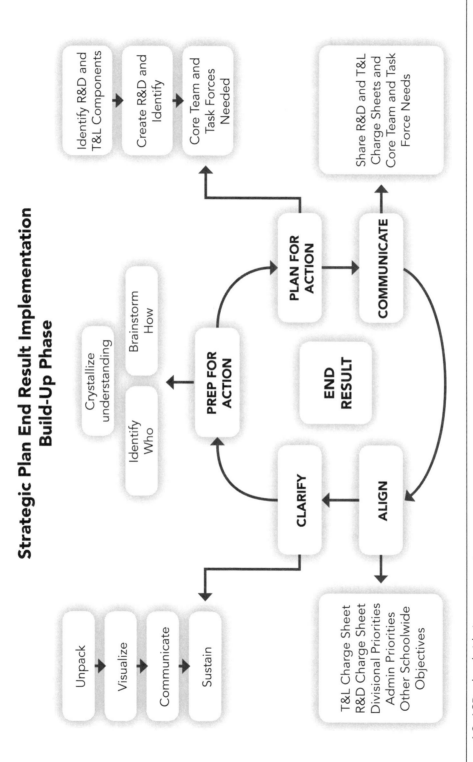

Figure 4.3: ASB schoolwide improvement process.

achievement and individualized learning through data-informed decision making.

2. **21st century skills**—ASB ensures student mastery of 21st century skills through standards, curriculum, instruction, assessment, professional development, and learning environments.

The T&L Core Team broke down each of these end results and formed task forces to study and develop a plan for implementation.

Individualized Learning

We decided to break the work on individualized learning into four components: (1) knowing our students very well, (2) improving our use of assessment for learning, (3) learning how to use assessment data to plan for differentiated instruction, and (4) building our repertoire of differentiated instruction. Our T&L Core Team divided itself into several different task forces so we could fully understand each component and develop a plan for our teachers to implement individualized learning.

21st Century Skills

After modifying the enGauge model (Bellanca & Brandt, 2010, pg. 58), we identified nine 21st century skills:

1. Collaboration
2. Critical thinking
3. Communication
4. Creativity and innovation
5. Managing complexity
6. Global awareness
7. Information fluency
8. Taking personal responsibility
9. Multicultural literacy

As we solidified ideas, the leadership team thought it was necessary for the board of trustees to understand the research, ideas, and concepts of a 21st century school. In 2011, we shared a comprehensive presentation with the whole board. The result was a shared understanding of the possible future and focus of teaching and learning for the school. The board, as business leaders in their own fields, understood the need for our school to position itself as a school for the future.

However, they asked pointed questions about implementation of our plans and sought assurances that the foundation of the superstruct would not falter. We shared how the foundation would be enhanced and how students would gain by focusing on these transdisciplinary skills, bringing in research from David A. Sousa (2006) and Daniel T. Willingham (2009).

With research to support developing 21st century skills, we had the full support of the board to move forward with curriculum development through a 21st century skills lens and had put in place a solid foundation for understanding the effects teaching and learning these skills would have on curriculum, assessment, and instruction. We developed a common understanding of what the 21st century skills were and how to teach and assess these skills through our weekly divisional professional development time.

The Research and Development Core Team

Nearly every day, you hear of a new tool, method, or approach that claims to aid the teacher and learning process. Embracing the new can both ensure that your practice remains current and diminish your effectiveness by constantly shifting the ground beneath your feet. In the 2011–2012 school year, the American School of Bombay made the commitment to move beyond what was merely trendy by establishing a Research and Development Team.

The ASB Research and Development Team studies, prototypes (when required), designs, and develops new teaching and learning environments for the 21st century. During the 2011–2012 school year, several R&D task forces, each facilitated by an R&D Core Team member, researched and reported on the following topics: blended learning, facilities design, individualized learning, games-based learning, project-based learning, green education, multi-aged classrooms, BYOD, and social technologies in the classroom. Their research, along with recommended next steps for each topic, were shared with the leadership team for consideration and further action.

The current work of the R&D Team focuses on project-based learning, gamification, mobile learning, and internships. The R&D team has also studied alternate school year calendars and recommended a balanced school year calendar along with prototyping an intersessions program. While we encourage tinkering with new and emerging tools to support teaching and learning, we are keen to build the internal capacity to determine what is a trend and what is truly a paradigm shift.

In addition, we have established an International Research Collaborative (IRC), which will study specific topics across international schools in the world. We are also launching the R&D Studio, a sandbox for emerging tools, methods, or learning approaches.

Time for Reflection

We were excited about moving our community toward a newer and more contemporary concept of schooling. We recognized that our teachers needed to contribute to an emerging view of 21st century schooling for our community and wanted to ensure that our faculty was prepared to engage with 21st century teaching and learning. However, we had significant work to do with our teachers in order for this to happen and believed we needed to put in place structures that supported both reflection and collaboration. A recurring comment from both teachers and administrators was the need for more meaningful reflection. Our school culture valued rapid accommodation to change, an open mindset, and the ability to be flexible and adaptable. We also were conscious that this atmosphere could promote superficial change or a sense of instability, and our intention was to build a culture that valued thoughtful reflection on practice. We wanted to build our collective skill in the ability to think deeply about our practice, formulate ideas about changes we needed to make, provide useful feedback and relevant questions to one another, and authentically engage in each other's professional growth.

We soon learned about Critical Friends Groups (CFGs) from the National School Reform Faculty (www.nsrfharmony.org)—a way to process and reflect on how our work was affecting student learning. CFGs are groups of educators carefully trained in the skills of reflecting on teaching in a spirit of inquiry and growth, with a heavy focus on student learning. These professional learning communities provided an effective context to understand our work with students, our relationships with peers, and our thoughts, assumptions, and beliefs about teaching and learning. We saw this as an excellent venue in which to cultivate our collective skills in the art of reflection. Faculty members were invited to spend a week obtaining CFG training from qualified consultants of the National School Reform Faculty. We realized with some surprise that we had hit a gold mine. A number of teams throughout the school quickly implemented the reflective practices and protocols for group work, and they had an immediate impact on the way in which colleagues interacted with one another around work and the quality of our conversations. The school remained committed over a three-year period to training a large number of teachers and administrators as CFG coaches qualified to lead CFGs across the school. These individuals play an important role in leading colleagues through the process of reflection to support our work toward school goals.

Revised Hiring Practices

We also adjusted our hiring practices to prepare our faculty to engage in 21st century teaching and learning. We made immediate shifts in our hiring rubric to add new skills that we believed were critical for teachers' success at ASB in our changing environment. Being innovative, collaborative, and reflective were three such skills. It was essential for teachers to have an open mindset to continual change but be reflective about what, how, and when to embrace change. Teachers were expected to have technology-integration skills and the ability to selectively choose tools that had the most significant impact on learning. Collaboration with others was essential to move our work forward; we were not interested in lone wolves. Additionally, teachers needed perseverance or grit, influence and motivation, critical thinking, and the ability to build relationships with others. Our process of identifying prospective teachers began shifting as we interviewed for these characteristics and attributes. Being clear on the mindset and skill set of teaching candidates may have been the single most important part of shifting our school. With teachers who wanted to come to a school that was moving to a new model of teaching and learning, we had the right people in the building to ensure that change would happen and would be sustainable.

We firmly believed that individuals with an open mindset could learn how to teach in new ways, and therefore our orientation and transition program for all new hires began to broaden to meet individual needs. Prior to new hires arriving at ASB, we sent them surveys to ascertain their strengths and areas for growth. Based on that information, we organized numerous workshops and training opportunities over the first few months of school. We offered weekly technology cafes, personal training on new software and digital tools, online courses, and onsite tech support. We also set up CFGs for all new faculty led by veteran ASB teachers to support and model how we work together. Through this professional development, we provided support and established positive relationships for future work. Our usual approach was to invite new teachers to join the Lausanne Learning Institute (www.lausannelearning.com), an educational technology conference held every summer. Our teachers benefited greatly from the variety of workshops about technology integration. Then, after over five years of having our new teachers attend this institute, we began to realize that our teachers needed a different kind of orientation—one more tailored to their individual needs and one that we felt teachers and administrators at our own school could better address. The level of expertise and skill that our own faculty possessed had evolved to the point that they could provide a high-quality orientation for incoming new colleagues. We began to bring new teachers to our school in April for a weeklong induction to working at ASB. We were well into another phase of our development.

Solid Foundation: 2012 and Beyond

At the beginning of the 2012–2013 school year, our dream became a reality. We moved into two new facilities: a brand-new elementary school and a completely overhauled secondary school. These thoroughly transformed teaching and learning environments were designed to foster creativity and collaboration and contained flexible spaces that allowed for small-group work and individualized learning. With movable walls and windows into learning spaces to showcase teaching and learning, teachers started to engage in thoughtful conversations about practice. Traditional grade-level and discipline silos dissipated, and our atmosphere of openness evolved. Additionally, a deeper reflection on our work arose as teachers leveraged their colleagues' instructional practices to best support student learning in the new learning spaces. This set the stage for our next evolution: superstruct 2.0.

Superstruct 2.0

After a year of intensive work on creating new structures for teacher collaboration and gaining greater understanding of 21st century skills and individualized learning than we ever imagined possible, we had a lot of excitement—and a lot of tired teachers. We re-evaluated what we wanted to and could accomplish and looked at how to focus the most immediate work: getting to know all of our students and supporting them on their learning journey. As a result, in the 2012–2013 school year, we aimed for simplicity, focus, and impact. We decided that in order for us to create a school based around individualizing learning, we would first focus on getting to know our students in a variety of ways and increasing our knowledge of how to best support all learners.

We began the year by having teachers develop an increased awareness of the impact of social and emotional learning on academic learning and on helping students become metacognitive learners by building understanding and tools for reflection on learning. In order to build this picture, we looked at a variety of student data, such as achievement on standardized tests, academic grades, and approaches to learning, which we keep in our student information system. We went further, looking at data on student involvement in after-school activities, the quantity of schools students had enrolled in during the past ten years, and the number of languages students spoke, again all accessible in our student information system. We also looked at teachers' observational records, shared at grade-level student-concerns meetings, and elicited parents' thoughts on their children, students' hopes and dreams for the future, and fears for the year through surveys at our open houses. By beginning the year here, we hoped to build the understanding that our students were living complex lives, and we had both opportunities and an obligation to ensure their success. We decided to support high-achieving students in particular in a way that mirrored the support we provided for struggling students.

We then began sharing what we do in classes in order to challenge these students. The two most prevalent strategies for high-achieving students were (1) having them tutor learners who did not have a solid grasp of concepts and (2) having them work independently on enrichment or extension work. We walked through what a day would be like for one of these high-achieving students and committed ourselves to providing more and better for them. Focusing in on differentiating for high-achieving students acted as a jumping-off point or model for individualizing learning for all students. In offering this challenge to our faculty, we also talked about using the expertise of the people at our school. We leaned on our literacy coach, who developed and shared resources for high-achieving students; a librarian, who worked with gifted-and-talented students in the past; academic support teachers, who modeled when and how to differentiate lessons; and a data and instruction coach, whose background was in mathematics instruction. The mantra became "work smarter" in order to meet the needs of all students. Teachers took up this call and since have been working collaboratively to build everything from minilessons to units with our experts in the building.

Targeted Skills

In addition to individualizing learning, we decided to focus on four of the nine targeted 21st century skills (see page 110). Divisional teaching and learning teams led professional development on how to intentionally teach and assess collaboration, creativity and innovation, critical thinking, and information fluency. Based on benchmarks developed by a T&L task force in the 2011–2012 school year, the divisional T&L teams created developmentally appropriate rubrics for each of the four skills. The elementary school worked to align the four skills with similar skills already articulated in the Primary Years Program (PYP). In middle school, in addition to developing rubrics and professional development for the four skills, we created an exploratory course called Creativity, Collaboration, and Critical Thinking. This course used the Destination Imagination team-building and problem-solving model to develop these skills in students (Destination Imagination, 2012). In high school, a team of teachers developed rubrics for 21st century skills. The teams shared and evaluated these rubrics in each department, and they are now being implemented across the curriculum. Our next steps in all divisions are to have teachers document in our curriculum maps which of the benchmarks underlying these four skills they are teaching and how they are doing this so that we can begin to align when, how, and to what degree we are preparing our students for their futures. Through this work on 21st century skills and the design of structures to meet students' needs, as well as through the possibilities our new facilities offer, we are primed to shift instruction to support student growth and to explore innovative instructional practices. We will continue to use a research and development framework to research and prototype these practices.

To remain aligned with our vision of superstructing, we are working to build instructional coaching capacity in our teachers so that we can bring in novice teachers, those in their first two years of teaching, as coteachers. This will allow more seasoned teachers to take time out of the classroom to work in new or different ways, such as facilitating professional development or researching and prototyping a new area of interest or passion.

Conclusion

Being invited to share the story of our journey encouraged us to consider our history and ponder the steps we took, decisions we made, and successes and failures we experienced. It has been a most illuminating process. In closing, in no particular order, we want to capture some of what we have learned about our journey.

- Our journey is messy and not linear. It is a process of discovery, and we did not start out with a completely clear and exact picture of what we were aiming for. We have notions of what we want, glimmers and ideas, some of them incomplete or unarticulated. There are some wrong turns and miscalculations. Some of our decisions were brilliant, and some have fallen short. Some of it is guesswork. But what has stood out for us is that we have maintained a culture of learning and an open mindset from all our experiences. As humans, we are attuned to learning from our experiences—babies do this from the minute they are born; it is a natural way that we make sense of our environment. Thus, we believe that even through our mistakes, we can learn, and if we intentionally build on what we've learned, we can do even better. This belief turns all experiences into a positive opportunity for learning.

- We have been proactive about change. We recognize that the world is changing very rapidly, and we embrace change as part of modern-day life. This means that we recognize that we will need to adjust ourselves to accept changes coming up. One way that we do this is by planning for change. We stay abreast of upcoming developments and look for potential emerging trends so that we will be prepared. Another way that we embrace change is by allowing ourselves the opportunity to change something if it isn't working, and to do so fairly quickly. Rather than being slow and rigid, we aim to be nimble and flexible to meet changing priorities. Our decision-making approach isn't to set things in stone, nor is it to change irresponsibly. Instead, we allow ourselves the freedom to consider new information that may call for different decisions.

- We navigate between the 30,000-foot strategic view and the 5,000-foot operational view. Both views are important but even more critical is the ability to navigate between them when necessary. It is important for us to make long-term strategic plans, looking at overall structures and systems to plan and measure impact. It is equally important that we pay attention to the truth about how things are really working on a day-to-day basis on the ground. Knowing when to apply a long- or a short-term perspective is a highly valued skill in our school.

- We pay attention. Knowing that technology is developing very quickly, we research the current best and latest digital tools, social media trends, and technological breakthroughs. It's not about the technology, it's about the learning, and we are constantly thinking of better ways to enhance our view of technology integration.

- We collaborate and share with others. We are always looking for ways to present our work and encourage others to do similar work. We are quite proactive in identifying people who will inspire others. We welcome feedback in all its forms. We don't know everything, and we need others to weigh in and share their ideas and suggestions with us.

- We regularly invite feedback. We are not afraid of feedback and appreciate all the help we can get. We have a flat organization in which anyone can share ideas through brainstorming and problem solving. We listen to and respect each other, and we are risk takers who take temporary failures in stride.

- We read! We speak the same language with each other because we read many of the same books and articles as we continue to cull best practices from all over. We help each other understand key ideas, and we ponder the same difficult-to-answer questions.

- We include our students in the process, listening to them and respecting their real-life experiences and insights. They have helped us to let go of approaches that were originally promising but did not pan out, and they have found unexpected uses for other tools.

The American School of Bombay continues to thrive through various changes and developments every year. We remain focused on an ambitious strategic plan that we revisit regularly, and new developments continue to invigorate and strengthen us.

References and Resources

American School of Bombay. (2006). *American School of Bombay strategic plan 2006–2011*. Mumbai, Maharashtra, India: Author.

American School of Bombay. (2008). *IT vision statement*. Accessed at https://sites .google.com/a/asbindia.org/valecha/it-vision-statement on September 15, 2013.

American School of Bombay. (2011). *American School of Bombay strategic plan 2011–2016*. Mumbai, Maharashtra, India: Author.

Bellanca, J., & Brandt, R. (Eds.). (2010). *21st century skills: Rethinking how students learn*. Bloomington, IN: Solution Tree Press.

Burkhardt, G., Monsour, M., Valdez, G., Gunn, C., Dawson, M., Lemke, C., et al. (2003). *enGauge 21st Century Skills: Literacy in the digital age*. Naperville, IL: North Central Regional Educational Laboratory.

Christensen, C. M., Johnson, C. W., & Horn, M. B. (2008). *Disrupting class: How disruptive innovation will change the way the world learns*. New York: McGraw-Hill.

Clay, M. M. (2006). *An observation survey of early literacy achievement* (2nd ed.). Portsmouth, NH: Heinemann.

Collins, J. (2001). *Good to great: Why some companies make the leap . . . and others don't*. New York: Harper Business.

Cooper, D. (2007). *Talk about assessment: Strategies and tools to improve teaching and learning*. Scarborough, Ontario, Canada: Thomson Nelson.

Destination Imagination. (2012). *Roadmap: A course guide for team managers*. Accessed at www.fldi.org/index.php/news/258-destination-imagination-offers-new -resource-for-team-managers.html on September 22, 2013.

Dweck, C. (2006). *Mindset: The new psychology of success*. New York: Ballantine Books.

Fountas, I. C., & Pinnell, G. S. (2007). *Benchmark Assessment System 1*. Portsmouth, NH: Heinemann. Accessed at www.heinemann.com/fountasandpinnell/BAS1 _Overview.aspx on April 1, 2013.

Gladwell, M. (2000). *The tipping point: How little things can make a big difference*. New York: Little, Brown.

Gladwell, M. (2005). *Blink: The power of thinking without thinking.* New York: Little, Brown.

Gladwell, M. (2008). *Outliers: The story of success.* New York: Little, Brown.

Guskey, T. R. (Ed.). (2009). *Practical solutions for serious problems in standards-based grading.* Thousand Oaks, CA: Corwin Press.

Independent School Management. (2010). *Special collection: The 21st century school.* Wilmington, DE: Author.

International Baccalaureate. (2013). *Middle Years Programme curriculum: Areas of interaction.* Accessed at www.ibo.org/myp/curriculum/interaction/approaches on September 20, 2013.

International Society for Technology in Education (ISTE). (2008). *NETS·T.* Accessed at www.iste.org/docs/pdfs/nets-t-standards.pdf?sfvrsn=2 on April 1, 2013.

Jacobs, H. H. (Ed.). (2010). *Curriculum 21: Essential education for a changing world.* Alexandria, VA: Association for Supervision and Curriculum Development.

Johnson, L., Adams, S., & Haywood, K. (2011). *NMC Horizon Report: 2011 K–12 edition.* Austin, TX: New Media Consortium. Accessed at http://media.nmc.org /iTunesU/HR-K12/2011/2011-Horizon-Report-K12.pdf on April 2, 2013.

Johnson, L., Levine, A., Smith, R., & Smythe, T. (2009). *The 2009 Horizon Report: K–12 edition.* Austin, TX: New Media Consortium.

Kegan, R., & Lahey, L. L. (2009). *Immunity to change: How to overcome it and unlock potential in yourself and your organization.* Boston: Harvard Business School Press.

Kirchner, M. (2010, September 24). *Explore the world of Superstruct.* Accessed at http://iftf.org/future-now/article-detail/explore-the-world-of-superstruct on April 1, 2013.

McGonigal, J. (2009). *You know you're superstructing when.* . . . Accessed at http:// janemcgonigal.files.wordpress.com/2010/12/strategy-matrix-card_reader-1.pdf on September 15, 2013.

McGonigal, J. (2011). *Reality is broken: Why games make us better and how they can change the world.* New York: Penguin Press.

Northwest Evaluation Association. (2013). *Measures of academic progress.* Accessed at www.nwea.org/products-services/assessments/map%C2%AE on September 16, 2013.

Pausch, R. (2008). *The last lecture.* New York: Hyperion.

Pink, D. (2009). *Drive: The surprising truth about what motivates us.* New York: Riverhead Books.

Reeves, D. B. (2011). *Elements of grading: A guide to effective practice.* Bloomington, IN: Solution Tree Press.

Senge, P. (1990). *The fifth discipline: The art and practice of the learning organization.* New York: Doubleday.

Sousa, D. A. (2006). *How the brain learns* (3rd ed.). Thousand Oaks, CA: Corwin Press.

Wiggins, G., & McTighe, J. (2005). *Understanding by design* (2nd ed.). Alexandria, VA: Association for Supervision and Curriculum Development.

Willingham, D. T. (2009). *Why don't students like school?* San Francisco: Jossey-Bass.

 **Brandon L. Wiley, EdD,** is the executive director of the Asia Society's International Studies Schools Network (ISSN), a design-driven network of over thirty public, charter, and independent schools located in eight states. ISSN is focused on supporting the development of internationally focused schools that empower students to be globally competent and college and career ready. Brandon coordinates the efforts of a U.S. team of consultants while assisting district and school leaders in implementing the ISSN model and Graduation Performance System.

Before joining the Asia Society, Brandon served as the assistant superintendent for curriculum and instruction in the West Seneca Central School District. With experience as a classroom teacher, director of staff development, and district-level administrator, Brandon offers practical experience in implementing school and district reforms and innovative programs. He is a frequent blogger and sought-after speaker focusing on school reform, globalization, and school innovation. For more information about Brandon's work, follow him on Twitter @bwileyone.

To book Brandon L. Wiley for professional development, contact pd@solution -tree.com.

Chapter 5

Leading for Global Competence: A Schoolwide Approach

By Brandon L. Wiley

If you had to close your eyes and picture what success in schools should look, sound, and feel like, what would you envision? Would you picture students from different cultures working collaboratively, speaking multiple languages, and over-coming barriers of time and geography to accomplish their goals? Would you see students self-aware, self-motivated, and flexible in their thinking? Perhaps you would see students who are sensitive to the needs of others, who take action to solve complex problems and have a natural disposition to make the world a better place? Students like Eliza, a graduating senior at the Denver Center for International Studies, who shared the following:

> It is undeniable that the globally-focused education I received has prepared me for the challenges I will face both in college and eventually in my career. There are not enough people in the world today who are passionate about enacting global change and have the facilities and capabilities to do so. Going to my school taught me that it is not enough to simply understand world issues, you have to take action to rectify them. (Personal communication, E. Cummings, 2013)

These are not naive fantasies but tangible hopes for what schools of the 21st century can and should strive to represent.

Schools that focus on fostering the 21st century literacies must depart from the industrial model, where outcomes and success are defined in very limited ways. A culture of standardized testing, rote memorization, limited student engagement, and a focus on basic skills acquisition are the norm in far too many schools. Preparing students with the skills, knowledge, and dispositions that will allow them to be successful in life should not be a lofty goal. It is, in fact, the promise made to every student who enters our school doors from the earliest age.

Although the responsibility to create a learning environment that promotes this type of success falls to school leaders and teachers every day, in every corner of the world, agreeing on what success looks like in the 21st century may conjure debate and speculation. Do test scores or grade point averages define success? Graduation rates or the number of students enrolled in postsecondary programs? As you can see, Eliza has a very clear definition of what constitutes success for her own life.

At the heart of preparing students to be globally competent is a desire to help them develop the skills and mindset necessary to compete, collaborate, and adapt in a changing world. By helping students investigate questions of local and global significance, understand various perspectives, communicate with diverse audiences, and take action to make a difference, schools prepare them for a world that is yet to be defined. This stance is quite different than the traditional belief that schools should teach a body of knowledge and expect students to perform on a set of uniform measures. Instead, it promotes the importance of curiosity, creativity, and innovation. It fuels students to want to understand the world around them more deeply with the hope of making it better than it currently is (Mansilla & Jackson, 2011).

While the term *global* may seem abstract or vague, schools around the world have begun to put concrete structures and practices in place to enable students to develop global competence, defined as the capacity and disposition to understand and act on issues of global significance. The four competencies or domains (figure 5.1, page 136) are students' ability to (1) investigate the world beyond their immediate environment, (2) recognize others' perspectives and their own, (3) communicate ideas effectively with diverse audiences, and (4) take action to improve conditions (Mansilla & Jackson, 2011). Through clear and purposeful leadership from both classroom teachers and school leaders alike, the school can gain an intentional focus on what global looks, sounds, and feels like. Schools can transform curriculum, instruction, assessment, and organization by developing a coherent vision and strategy to make global education and the incorporation of these four competencies a focus in your school.

The intent of this chapter is to provide explicit examples from schools around the world that are infusing global competence into their everyday practices. There is no cookie-cutter approach, nor is there a *best way* for this to occur. In many cases, global competence begins with one teacher or a group of teachers who are passionate about opening their classroom doors to the world. I refer to *leadership* in the broadest sense possible. Leadership in schools can and should come from a variety of players—teachers, principals, students, and parents. It is the collective effort of all these constituents that truly maximizes a school's potential. However, the building administrator is likely the primary actor who can enable many of these practices and changes to occur.

Asia Society

Many of the examples will come from the work I am most familiar with as the director of the Asia Society's International Studies Schools Network. Since 1956, the international nonprofit Asia Society, founded by American philanthropist John D. Rockefeller III, has worked to bring about a shared future between the nations of Asia and the United States. The Asia Society is a global and pan-Asian organization working to strengthen relationships and promote understanding among the people, leaders, and institutions of the United States and Asia. More specifically, the organization serves as a connector, convener, and catalyst for discussion and innovation in the areas of the arts, business, policy, and education. For many years, the Asia Society's education department focused on the development of high-quality curriculum and content material about Asia for use in U.S. schools. However, shortly after the events of September 11, 2001, the organization began to take stock of the impact it was having on the field. Over the course of several years and under the leadership of Michael Levine, Vivien Stewart, and Anthony Jackson, the education department began to focus its attention on creating resources and opportunities to help U.S. schools develop their students' global competence.

Through the support of the Bill and Melinda Gates Foundation, the Asia Society partnered with several large urban school districts, the New York City Department of Education, the Los Angeles Unified School District, and the Charlotte-Mecklenburg Schools to create ten small, internationally themed secondary schools. The concept was to develop schools whose mission and purpose was to prepare high school graduates to be both globally competent and college and career ready. Since 2003, the Asia Society has worked in partnership with these and other school districts, charter authorities, and nonpublic schools to create the International Studies Schools Network (ISSN), a network of over thirty design-driven schools across the United States. Over a ten-year period, the ISSN has not only helped to create a number of new public schools in urban locations but has also partnered with existing schools in suburban and rural communities that are seeking to transform their educational approach and outcomes for students. While the network has diversified with respect to the types of schools and geographic locations it represented, approximately 80 percent of all students served are minority, and 63 percent are from low-income families. In 2012, about 90 percent of our students graduated on time, with over 85 percent continuing on to postsecondary education.

The good news for school leaders and teachers is that you don't need to belong to a network like the ISSN or spend a great deal of money to globalize your school. You must, however, be intentional about your actions and attempt to create coherence within your school around the notion of global competence. The remainder of this chapter outlines six strategies you can use to do so.

Strategy One: Make the Case

Almost every school you walk into has a mission statement. It may be emblazoned on a plaque hanging in the main office or highlighted on the school website. Wherever the mission is displayed, the true test happens when you walk down the halls and visit classrooms. To what extent does the school personify that mission? Put differently, is everyone aware, invested, and committed to ensuring that the words on the plaque are actually realized? Unfortunately, in many schools not only is the mission ambiguous but the behaviors of the adults and students do not support or help actualize that mission. At other times, the "initiative of the day" or the latest mandate imposed on the school dilute the mission.

Developing a globally focused mission and vision is a critical first step in globalizing learning for students. All constituents must have an understanding of why students need to be globally competent for their future success, and that understanding does not arise without effort. Being global goes far beyond cultural festivals, flags hanging in the hallways, or family nights featuring international cuisine. Schools that have made a compelling case for global competence consistently use their vision, mission, and shared beliefs to guide daily decisions. They engage the community in the development of a mission statement that puts value on engaging, real-world learning and college readiness. When a school has a shared and fully realized mission, the mission is reflected in all aspects of that school, including its policies, culture, and quality of instruction.

The Elevator Pitch

Before creating a vision or mission, school leaders must develop their own *elevator pitch* when talking about the importance of global competence. Framing the importance of preparing students to thrive in an increasingly global society is paramount when school leaders speak to teachers, students, parents, or community members. In their chapter "Educating for Global Competence: Redefining Learning for an Interconnected World" in *Mastering Global Literacy* (Jacobs,

TWO SAMPLE MISSIONS OR VISION STATEMENTS

Ambassador School of Global Leadership

The vision of the Ambassador School of Global Leadership (ASGL) is to produce globally competent citizens who are prepared to meet all of the challenges of the 21st century. ASGL strives to create an environment for learning and development, in which every student is prepared to succeed in college, other post secondary education, or work and compete, communicate, and cooperate within an interconnected global community. Through this process, we facilitate the ability to embrace diversity and engage responsibly in the ongoing and emerging issues of the world with compassion, empathy, and tolerance. (Ambassador School of Global Leadership, n.d.)

Denver Center for International Studies

Denver Center for International Studies (DCIS) at Montbello prepares students in grades 6–12 for college, career, and life by helping them understand how to seize the countless opportunities the world has to offer. By graduation, every DCIS at Montbello student will be multilingual, interculturally competent, and prepared to solve problems and lead communities worldwide with knowledge and compassion.

To empower and equip students to thrive in our increasingly complex world, DCIS at Montbello offers a globally minded approach to education that combines rigorous academics, intercultural interaction, public service, travel opportunities, and extracurricular activities that are a whole lot of fun. Our students are specially prepared to tackle 21st-century challenges because they are outstanding communicators. DCIS at Montbello students receive intensive instruction in world languages and the creation and use of technology. They are regularly challenged to hone their communication skills through collaborative public-service projects at our school, in our city, across our nation—and around the world. (Denver Center for International Studies at Montbello, n.d.)

2014), Tony Jackson and Veronica Boix Mansilla (2014) make a very sound case as to why schools should put a greater focus on preparing students to be globally competent. Among their arguments, they explain the changing nature of the world economic stage and the type of skills students will need to be competitive. According to the Committee for Economic Development (2006), U.S. employers will "increasingly need employees with knowledge of foreign languages and cultures" to work effectively with partners around the globe (p. 2). The nature of work itself is also changing. As more routine jobs become automated through technology or outsourced to cheaper labor markets, the economic advantage will go to people who can analyze and solve problems, recognize patterns and similarities, and communicate and interact with other people, especially those who do not share the same culture.

However, globalization is about more than employment. Virtually every major issue people face—from global warming to terrorism—has an international dimension. Communities throughout North America have reflected world trends in migration and immigration, generating enormous cultural and linguistic diversity in our schools. Meeting this challenge is necessary not only for the economic prosperity of our students but also their personal satisfaction and happiness as adults.

Student Voice

Besides all of these external factors, it is important to consider another voice in this discussion—the students.' Students are looking for meaningful, authentic learning experiences that ground them in the world. Yet evidence suggests that many of our schools are not engaging them in these ways. Take, for example, a 2012 World Savvy study. Since 2002, World Savvy has developed programs that address the critical need for youth to acquire global knowledge and 21st century skills. In their estimation, many K–12 education systems are not addressing the need to prepare students for an interconnected world and the increasingly diverse communities in which they live. Utilizing the *World Savvy Global Competency Survey*, they probed into the skills, knowledge, values, and behaviors of students between the ages of eighteen and twenty-four, all of whom had graduated from high school or earned a GED, to gauge the degree of global competency of the average U.S. high school graduate. Not only did the results highlight the perceived gap found in K–12 education, it also suggested a high demand among young adults for global competency education (World Savvy, 2012).

According to the study's findings:

- Eighty-six percent of those surveyed say they agree that a solid foundation in world history and events is crucial to coming up with solutions to problems in the world today.

- Six in ten say they would be better employees if they had a better understanding of different world cultures.

- Nearly nine in ten believe that developments abroad can have significant implications on the U.S. economy.

- Seventy-nine percent say that it is important in today's world to be comfortable interacting with people of different cultural backgrounds (on par with the perceived importance of writing skills [78 percent]), technical skills [76 percent], and math skills [77 percent]).

- Eighty percent believe that jobs are becoming increasingly international in nature. (World Savvy, 2012).

Despite this desire to develop global competence in school, respondents reported that a majority of their schools did not support this type of learning. Only 12 percent of respondents say they "agree completely" that in their sixth- to twelfth-grade education they received instruction that helps them to understand the roots of global issues that affect their current lives. The study also suggested that students who had regular exposure to a global curriculum and focus on world issues were more inclined to take part in their local communities, seek out information about local and world events, and vote. A majority of respondents expressed a wish that their schools had taken more of a global than a national view of instruction (World Savvy, 2012).

Challenges to Making the Case

Even though we know the importance of preparing students to be globally competent, and data suggest students want this focus, many schools still have not made the commitment to promote this type of learning. There may be several reasons for this gap. Harvard scholar Fernando Reimers, one of the foremost experts on global education, contends that two obstacles typically stand in the way of a school promoting global competence—lack of resources and an obsolete mindset (Reimers, 2009). As schools and systems try to deal with competing initiatives and reduced resources, they push global competence, not traditional literacies, to the back burner. Furthermore, the traditional focus on literacy, numeracy, and science is more reflective of a compartmentalized way of thinking and does not lend itself to the more interdisciplinary approach of global competency. In a survey Reimers conducted with 150 school principals, he asked if there were opportunities for students to develop global competency in their school. More than half of the respondents said "not much" or "not at all" (Reimers, 2009). This, of course, only confirms what the students have also reported.

Perhaps another basic reason for this gap is that many school leaders and teachers themselves have not been taught global competency. If you have not been taught content using a global perspective or by connecting a topic to a globally significant issue, you may not think of doing so in your everyday practice. Providing teachers with a concrete example of global competence in action shows how it does not diminish instruction but, in fact, can add rigor. The Asia

Society (http://asiasociety.org/education), TakingITGlobal (www.tigweb.org), and Primary Source (www.primarysource.org) offer a variety of rich resources and lesson ideas for all content areas.

In conversations with school leaders, I'm often struck by their notion that bringing a global perspective to school is an add-on, or something to get to when everything else is done. Another common obstacle is the reality of too many competing initiatives within a school at one time. For example, many school leaders are attempting to help teachers implement the Common Core State Standards, teacher effectiveness frameworks, and a number of other locally driven initiatives. The extent to which a school leader is able to demonstrate how teaching for global competence helps address these other initiatives and provide coherence for his or her staff is a critical factor in implementing a global stance in a school.

LEADER ACTION STEPS

- Engage all stakeholders to develop a shared mission and vision that supports global competence.
- Develop your elevator pitch. Determine how you will make the case for global competence, including how it ties to school and district initiatives.
- Begin to educate your community about global competence and the types of skills students will need beyond high school through community forums, board of education presentations, or World Café (www.theworldcafe.com) events.
- With your faculty, share resources about global education, such as *Education Week's Global Learning* blog (http://blogs.edweek .org/edweek/global_learning); articles from the Asia Society website such as "Global Competence: Prepare Youth to Engage with the World" (http://asiasociety.org/education/partnership -global-learning/making-case/global-competence-prepare-youth -engage-world); and links to global resources on the EdSteps website (www.edsteps.org).
- Engage students in advocating for more globally focused instruc- tion in your school.

Strategy Two: Define Success

What would an entire school focused on preparing students for the world look like? How would it be structured? What type of learning would take place in such a school? These were the essential questions that guided the original development of our ISSN school design. The team at the Asia Society began its research by conducting visits to high-performing international studies schools around the United States and Canada, such as the International School of the Americas in San Antonio, Texas; the Eugene International High School in Eugene, Oregon; and the Washington International School in Washington, D.C., in a quest to define what exactly would need to happen in a school to ensure that students developed their global competence. Team members catalogued the type of instruction they found, how teachers assessed student learning, the structures that supported learning, and the types of partnerships that helped schools develop students' global competence. Throughout their travels, one element stood out—the mission of every ISSN school must be to create an environment for learning and exploration in which every student has the opportunity and support to develop the skills necessary to succeed in college or in other postsecondary options. Additionally, the goal of every ISSN school—to prepare students to understand the world and how it works by learning *in* and *with* the world—would serve as the foundation for success.

To achieve this mission, the ISSN began with a definition of what success looks like. The result is a profile of an Asia Society International Studies Schools Network high school graduate (Asia Society, 2012a).

- ISSN graduates are ready for college. They:
    - Earn a high school diploma by completing a college-preparatory, globally focused course of study requiring the demonstration of college-level work across the curriculum
    - Have the experience of achieving expertise by researching, understanding, and developing new knowledge about a world culture or an internationally relevant issue
    - Learn how to manage their own learning by identifying options, evaluating opportunities, and organizing educational experiences that will enable them to work and live in a global society
    - Graduate with all options open for postsecondary education, work, and service
- ISSN graduates have the knowledge required in the global era. They understand:
    - Mathematics as a universal way to make sense of the world; solve complex, authentic problems; and communicate their understandings using mathematical symbols, language, and conventions

- Critical scientific concepts, engage in scientific reasoning, and apply the processes of scientific inquiry to understand the world and explore possible solutions to global problems

- How the geography of natural and human-made phenomena influences cultural development, as well as historical and contemporary world events

- The history of major world events and cultures and utilize this understanding to analyze and interpret contemporary world issues

- Art and literature and use them as lenses through which to view nature, society, and culture, as well as to express ideas and emotions

- ISSN graduates are skilled for success in a global environment. They:

  - Are literate for the 21st century and proficient in reading, writing, viewing, listening, and speaking in English and in one or more other world languages

  - Demonstrate creative- and complex-thinking and problem-solving skills by analyzing and producing viable solutions to problems with no known or single right answer

  - Use digital media and technology to access and evaluate information from around the world and effectively communicate, synthesize, and create new knowledge

  - Make healthy decisions that enhance their physical, mental, and emotional well-being

- ISSN graduates are connected to the world. They:

  - Effectively collaborate with individuals from different cultural backgrounds and seek out opportunities for intercultural teamwork

  - Analyze and evaluate global issues from multiple perspectives

  - Understand how the world's people and institutions are interconnected and how critical international economic, political, technological, environmental, and social systems operate interdependently across nations and regions

  - Accept the responsibilities of global citizenship and make ethical decisions and responsible choices that contribute to the development of a more just, peaceful, and sustainable world

Written to articulate what students would know and be able to do at the commencement level, the graduate profile identifies the attributes students should aspire to achieve. Undergirding the entire profile is the overriding belief that *all students* will be successful in acquiring the skills necessary to be globally competent and college and career ready. Maintaining high expectations is not enough, however. ISSN schools must also put certain supports and mechanisms in place to ensure success for all students. Schools that are able to develop their own graduate profile can design the types of instruction and supports necessary to scaffold all students to achieve those outcomes. Maintaining high expectations also means that students take an active role in goal setting and monitoring their progress. Student success is not left to the teacher alone or, worse yet, to chance.

Providing access to a college preparatory program of study is the first step in helping students toward global competence. High school graduation alone is not the goal. Providing rigorous learning experiences that allow students to produce college-ready work and include globally significant issues prepares them for the world in which they will work and live. They must also learn how to manage their learning, identifying strengths, weaknesses, and opportunities for exploration and growth. Helping students learn *how to learn*, including how to access, analyze, synthesize, and communicate information and ideas, is of greater importance than empowering them to guess correctly on a series of multiple-choice tests. In this model, schools still utilize standardized tests, but they do so in a way that allows them to create plans to address performance gaps and, in many cases, create individualized learning plans for those who are not on track for success. While success on standardized testing does still matter, it is not the ultimate or only goal. When reflecting on this shift, I'm reminded of the question, Are we preparing students for a *lifetime of tests* or for the *tests of life*? The answer is both but with greater emphasis on the latter.

LEADER ACTION STEPS

- Work collaboratively with your faculty to develop a graduate profile or adapt the ISSN profile of a graduate (pages 131–132) to define what success looks like for students by the time they leave your school.

- Engage faculty in conversations around high expectations and consistency.

- Facilitate collaborative assessment of student work to help faculty discuss expectations and what quality looks like.

- Promote a college-going culture through campus visits, college counseling, and information nights for families.

SCHOOL SPOTLIGHT: VAUGHN INTERNATIONAL STUDIES ACADEMY, PACOIMA, CALIFORNIA

Vaughn International Studies Academy (VISA) is the crown jewel of the Vaughn Next Century Learning Center, a network of charter campuses started by Yvonne Chan. Serving students in grades 9–12 in Pacoima, California, VISA is a shining example of what maintaining high expectations for students can mean, both for them and the local community. Located in a community rife with gang activity and a history of high school dropouts, VISA has provided a safe, nurturing, and supportive environment for students as a viable option to prepare them for college and careers. They do not set the bar low, however. The school requires students to take four years of Mandarin Chinese, provides rigorous coursework in STEAM (science, technology, engineering, arts, and mathematics), and exposes students to service and out-of-school learning. All of these learning experiences are viewed through a global lens and provide opportunities to investigate the world, weigh perspectives, communicate ideas, and take action. VISA has proven that setting high expectations, providing supports to catch students before they fail, and engaging the community in the process leads to positive outcomes. One additional indicator of success is continued academic growth and improvement on state assessments each year since the school has opened. By drawing students from the impoverished neighborhoods of Pacoima, San Fernando, and Sylmar, the school has left an indelible mark on its students and has been a positive influence on transforming the local community.

Strategy Three: Make Strategic Upgrades

The major shift necessary in most schools to promote global competence comes in the areas of curriculum, instruction, and assessment. Creating schools that are more student-centered and focused on personalization will be the hallmark of the 21st century. With the advent of online courses, virtual schools, and massive open online courses (MOOCs), we have seen that students do not need to come to the brick-and-mortar school to learn any longer. They are not waiting for their teachers to let them work with their peers, because they are already using social media to connect with peers halfway around the world. While there is still a great deal of inequity in achievement and opportunity in the world, the world our students will inherit will require a heavy reliance on self-motivation, self-sufficiency, and self-actualization. The one-size-fits-all approach that the traditional education system has built will no longer produce enough students who can think at higher levels, solve problems creatively, and innovate for the future.

Creating blended learning environments, where students can engage in learning online and in person, will be in greater demand as technology improves. The perpetuation of requiring seat-time mandates and shackling students to their schools needs to evolve into greater opportunities for internships, service learning, and community-based inquiry. Providing multiple pathways for students will allow them to develop at their own pace and according to their own interests. Critics will argue that this is not sustainable or cost effective. Others will complain that it will require changes in both policy and practice for too many of our schools. To be competitive and productive citizens, students in the 21st century must be flexible and innovative. So, too, should the schools that develop them.

For a school leader, the challenge of creating an adaptive learning environment can be overwhelming. I would offer that it comes through gradual, purposeful upgrades to your curriculum, instruction, and assessment framework. Rome wasn't built in a day! Developing students' global competence is perhaps best achieved through a project-based curriculum, instruction, and assessment framework. Start with the assets you already have in place and identify the high-leverage changes that will move your learning environment closer to the innovative, globally focused program you seek. This next section will identify upgrades that you can make to the curriculum, instruction, and assessment framework in your school, as well as the types of learning experiences you can offer to students.

Curriculum

The primary framework schools should use when planning and developing curriculum is the framework for global competence (figure 5.1, page 136) that the Council of Chief State School Officers and the Asia Society developed (Mansilla & Jackson, 2011). Teachers must consider how and when they can provide opportunities for their students to investigate the world, recognize perspectives, communicate ideas, and take action in the classroom. While teachers must be aware of local, state, and national standards or curriculum requirements, they can easily apply this framework to any subject area. It starts by providing examples of what global competence looks like in each discipline area. For example, as a mathematics teacher, my goal is likely to help students think like a mathematician. How

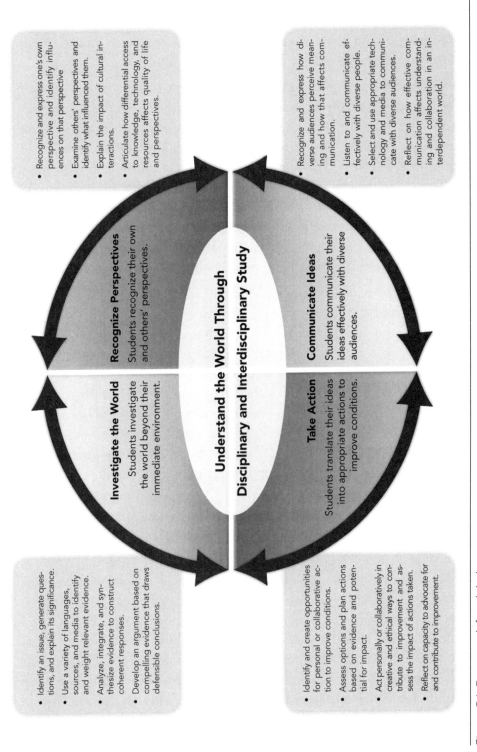

Figure 5.1: Framework for global competence.

Source: Reprinted with permission from Mansilla & Jackson, 2011.

do mathematicians use their skills and knowledge to communicate with one another? How might they use mathematics to take action or make a difference in the world? Is it possible that different people can look at the same data and come away with different understandings? These are the types of questions we must engage our teachers in when framing content.

One strategic upgrade in curriculum is to identify points where teachers can use globally significant issues to introduce or deepen content learning. The intent is not to teach everything all the time with global connections. That is not only unnecessary but can be exhausting. Teachers should instead consider their entire curriculum and attempt to make connections to global issues that are relevant and serve as entry points to content topics. Globally significant issues might include environmental sustainability, population growth, economic development, global conflict and cooperation, global health, and human rights. In almost every case, these issues are also interdisciplinary in nature and require deep knowledge and higher-level thinking to develop plausible arguments or solutions. To return to the mathematics classroom, a student might apply statistical analysis formulas to create a hypothesis about population growth in a third-world country and make recommendations to address resulting inequities. In the traditional classroom, those same formulas may have been taught in isolation, without context or a plausible application. The use of globally significant issues not only causes students to take a more active interest in the world but also provides them with authentic purpose and application for their learning.

It is a misnomer that teaching students to be globally competent focuses on the development of soft skills at the expense of deep content knowledge. Quite the opposite is true. To develop global competence, students must have a solid foundation in content knowledge. To investigate the world and weigh perspectives, they must be able to access key content, make decisions about its validity, and determine how to use the information. Unfortunately, the idea of promoting global learning is often an either–or proposition. How can you hold students to high expectations while covering large amounts of content knowledge *and* infusing instruction with globally significant issues? I would argue that, on the contrary, globally significant issues are the perfect entry point to engage students in any number of content topics. A shift must occur, however, from teachers worrying about covering content to teachers focusing on student learning and mastery, going deeper in fewer major concepts and topics. Unfortunately, many current assessment systems have not allowed teachers to feel as if they can afford to do this.

When making decisions about instructional time, teachers often face many challenges. Weighing the demands of external pressures (school, district, state, and community) and the needs of the students can sometimes pose problems for teachers. Over time, teachers should collaborate to map the various times throughout students' careers that they will be engaged in the four domains of global competence (see page 136) or in global issues. Some schools adopt a thematic or conceptual approach, with each grade level taking on a particular issue and addressing it throughout the year in each content area. For example, the freshman-level experience may focus on the issue of identity. For a semester or the entire year, students would engage in ongoing projects and learning that help them identify a greater sense of self and understand what makes people similar and different. They may engage in in-depth studies of specific cultures, including typical rituals, practices, and norms found within a cultural group, and examine those practices against their own lives. An essential question that might drive such an ongoing study might be, "What is the American identity?" This open-ended, debatable question allows students an opportunity to reflect throughout their study, making connections to what they have learned throughout the year and challenging their preconceived notions of themselves and those around them. Schools that curriculum map as a practice often embed the global themes and performance tasks that students will complete each year. This type of coherence helps prevent redundancies in the curriculum and eliminates gaps in the students' learning experience. Ultimately, the goal is to build on previous learning while increasing rigor from one level to the next.

Instruction

Schools that focus on developing global competence take into account the diverse learners in every class. Across the school, teachers use project-based learning, higher-order questioning, and inquiry-based instructional strategies and student needs, learning styles, interests, and standards to guide them. Classrooms provide opportunities for students to learn and apply discipline-specific methods of inquiry. Woven throughout the curriculum are instructional strategies that enable students to demonstrate productive habits of mind, which include problem-solving, creative- and generative-thinking skills, the capacity to analyze issues of international significance from multiple perspectives, and the ability to direct their own learning.

A globally focused school needs to reconsider the roles of teachers and students in the learning process. As we attempt to prepare students to engage in the world and take ownership of their learning, teachers must reconceptualize their role and move away from being lead instructor toward the role of co-learner or facilitator. The process begins with teachers developing the capacity to design and utilize globally focused learning activities that are authentic and student-centered and provide multiple opportunities to reach mastery. However, before this, hiring a highly qualified, diverse staff is helpful in giving the school a global focus. To promote diversity and unique perspectives, ISSN schools attempt to recruit faculty with varied backgrounds, both professionally and personally. Many ISSN schools have developed a teacher profile—a description of the type of educator they are looking for when hiring. The profile of an Asia Society ISSN teacher serves as a job description of sorts to highlight the types of skills, experiences, and dispositions of a valuable teaching staff. Visit **go.solution-tree.com/21stcenturyskills** for the complete profile, which includes the following characteristics (Asia Society, 2012b):

- They possess the knowledge required in the global era that serves student learning. Additionally, they:

    - Have a deep understanding of their individual content and connect their content area to authentic global issues and perspectives

    - Understand and stay up to date on world events, international issues, and global debates and help students gain understanding of these through daily interactions

    - Present balanced viewpoints on global issues and assist students in viewing issues from multiple perspectives

    - Have the capacity to integrate international content, issues, and perspectives into a standards-based curriculum

    - Understand that decisions made locally and nationally have international impact and that international trends and events affect local and national options

    - Are able or willing to learn to communicate in one or more languages other than English

    - Recognize, value, and respect the broad spectrum of ethnicities and cultures in the school community and teach students to collaborate effectively with individuals from different backgrounds

- They are skilled for success in a global environment. Additionally, they:

    - Demonstrate proficiency in and model the essential skills of reading, writing, comprehending, listening, speaking, and viewing of media necessary for student learning in their content area

    - Develop and present information in an articulate and persuasive manner, orally, in writing, and through digital media

- Use problem-solving skills to recognize and act on the needs of individual students, colleagues, and members of the school community
- Ask reflective questions about their practice and continue to be intellectually curious and demonstrate the habits of mind that lead to lifelong learning about their craft, their students, and their content
- Utilize new strategies to reach every student and find resources to maximize student learning
- Use an inquiry-based model of teaching that enables students to actively manipulate ideas in order to construct knowledge, solve problems, and develop their own understanding of the content
- Use instructional strategies to draw on the diverse cultural assets among students, families, and communities
- Use multiple forms of assessment and instructional strategies to evaluate ongoing student learning, monitor and accelerate student progress to higher levels of performance, and motivate students to manage their own achievement
- Create opportunities for students to analyze and reflect on their own learning and provide feedback about their learning experiences

- They are connected to the world. Additionally, they:
  - Are proficient in the use of essential digital media and communications technologies and use them to communicate and work across national and regional boundaries
  - Appreciate and respect diversity and work effectively with people from other cultures, backgrounds, and fields of expertise
  - Have traveled internationally or are willing to engage in international learning experiences
- They prepare all students to be ready for college and careers in the global age. Additionally, they:
  - Design and implement a college-preparatory, globally focused course of study for students that systematically builds students' capacity to demonstrate college-level work across the curriculum
  - Recognize the levels of students' literacy in academic and social language and help them build meaningful bridges between the two

- Facilitate learning opportunities that enable students to have the experience of achieving expertise by researching, understanding, and developing new knowledge about a world culture or an internationally relevant issue

- Model and explicitly teach students how to manage their own learning by identifying options, evaluating opportunities, and organizing educational experiences that will enable them to work and live in a global society

In addition to examining the role teachers play in the instructional process, schools must put greater emphasis on the role of student voice. Schools that want their students to be globally competent should provide them with a role in the development of course content and the direction of their learning. School leaders can use formal and informal structures to solicit student input and make connections between course content and current world events and to identify areas for interconnected research and study. Student input about what to learn, how to learn it, and how to demonstrate learning can be incorporated into the curriculum design.

Assessment

There are no standardized tests to measure a student's global competence. Indeed, globally competent students must demonstrate an array of higher-order skills and the application of knowledge to real-world issues and problems. Assessment of student learning happens throughout the entire learning process. As a precursor to designing and scaffolding instructional activities, teachers must *backward plan* (Wiggins & McTighe, 2005), determining what students must know and be able to do and which assessment strategies will demonstrate that learning. When developing curriculum, teachers must embed formative assessments throughout the learning to ensure that students are on track and are provided multiple opportunities for feedback.

When designing high-quality summative assessments, another framework teachers might consider is SAGE (*student* choice, *authentic* context, *global* significance, and *exhibition* to an audience (Asia Society, 2012c):

- **Student choice**—The task calls on students to plan and assess their work over time through reflection. Students make key decisions about the direction of their work, focus, and presentation. To support this, the task provides opportunities for teachers to deliver formative and summative feedback to the students throughout the learning process. Strategies include:

- Choosing a topic, theme, problem, or global issue

- Creating a hypothesis

- Selecting a person in the field to conduct research with

- Choosing a final assessment or product (slide show, text, or documentary film)

- **Authentic context**—The task provides an experience that resembles what adults do in the real world. Students are asked to communicate, collaborate, think critically, be creative, negotiate with other people, and use digital media in ways that support knowledge building. Strategies include:

  - Creating a piece of technical writing (for example, an instruction manual or how-to text)

  - Creating a piece of advertising or media for a marketing campaign (such as a flier, public service announcement, commercial, or website)

  - Curating an exhibition

  - Creating a prototype

  - Developing a business plan or a funding proposal

- **Global significance**—The task fosters the capacity and dispositions to understand and act on issues of global significance. Students investigate the world as a means to problem solve genuine situations. Ideally, the task stimulates students to build knowledge that is cross-disciplinary. Strategies include:

  - Reading texts by global authors

  - Studying a text to identify elements of culture used by the author or to discuss how the text has influenced culture

  - Collaborating on projects with students around the globe (for example, Flat Classroom Project or iEARN—see page 153)

  - Creating a "think globally, act locally" service learning project

  - Reading a nonfiction text such as *The World Is Flat* (Friedman, 2005); *Guns, Germs, and Steel* (Diamond, 1999); *Multicultural Manners* (Dresser, 2005)

- **Exhibition to an audience**—The task provides students with opportunities to showcase or present their work to an appropriate and relevant audience beyond the teacher and classroom. Students are provided opportunities to discuss their work and receive feedback that holds them accountable for their claims. Strategies include:

- Present to a group who can support the idea (for example, the city council, principal, school board, teachers, parent groups, or nonprofit or business group).

- Publish in a magazine or online forum.

- Participate in a museum or library exhibition or a film festival.

The driving force behind the curriculum, assessment, and instruction model in ISSN schools is the Graduation Performance System (GPS). GPS supports an interdisciplinary, project-based approach, where teachers implement curriculum modules that last anywhere from one to three weeks at strategic points in the curriculum. In addition to the ISSN graduate profile, the Asia Society has developed a set of content-specific performance outcomes, as well as crosscutting performance outcomes for global leadership. We have also designed rigorous rubrics to ensure that students are truly progressing toward college readiness and global competence. These curriculum modules align the Common Core State Standards with the Asia Society's content-specific performance outcomes and graduate profile. These standards-based curricula are organized around enduring understandings and essential questions that reflect the four domains of global competence (figure 5.1, page 136). Each year, grade-level or interdisciplinary teams write new or refine existing course units to strengthen the global focus of the curriculum and deepen its connection to the ISSN graduate profile and performance outcomes. The faculty collaborates to align courses within and across grade-level teams and disciplines and, when appropriate, with out-of-school partners to provide well-articulated interdisciplinary and real-world connections.

The GPS performance cycle (figure 5.2, page 144) outlines the ongoing, recursive nature of the work. After teachers have designed curriculum modules that address standards, performance outcomes, and global significance, they implement the module and performance tasks resulting in student work. Once the work has been scored and feedback provided to students, they may choose items to include in their portfolios that demonstrate proficiency.

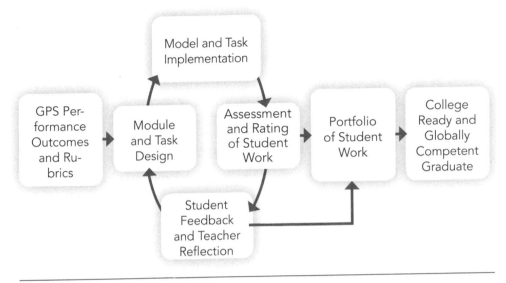

Figure 5.2: GPS performance cycle.

Because no one assessment can gauge a student's global competence, the collection of student work over time has proven to be a more authentic measure of growth and proficiency than any one standardized test. In many ISSN schools, for example, students develop and annually present a cumulative portfolio that demonstrates their reflective thinking or growth and the outcomes defined in the graduate profile (page 131) and GPS performance outcomes, which are a set of standards for global competence. In most cases, the school-based system for portfolio management is digital. Schools that commit to the use of a portfolio clearly communicate that student work and reflections are equally significant to other performance measures, such as standardized test scores. Although ISSN schools do not ignore standardized test scores, they also measure student achievement through public, communitywide exhibitions of portfolios or during student-led parent conferences.

In addition to portfolios, many schools utilize international capstone projects as a culminating activity that enables students to demonstrate expertise on an international issue, region of the world, or topic in which they are interested. Students select most capstone projects themselves based on their interests and highlight skills that demonstrate they are college ready. In many ISSN schools, capstones have replaced the traditional senior thesis or have required students to complete several smaller projects as a graduation requirement.

SCHOOL SPOTLIGHT: DENVER CENTER FOR INTERNATIONAL STUDIES, DENVER, COLORADO

Passages is a unique part of the DCIS curriculum that uses an outcomes-based approach, requiring students to develop individualized learning goals and design several research-based projects. These projects, which focus on international or intercultural topics, bring together a variety of skills and learning outcomes.

In her written reflections, DCIS teacher Darlene Rivera (Reflection entry, June 2012) describes the experience in the following way:

"Beginning in their junior year, students are challenged to test and develop high-level skills with research, writing, goal setting, time management, and leadership to obtain a deep understanding of an international or intercultural topic about which they are passionate. The academic rigor of Passages I focuses on the research and writing process that will enable students to succeed in college and in life. Its end product is a fifteen-page college-ready research paper that must connect to the DCIS graduate profile characteristics. Passages II and III require students to engage in an experiential learning activity that brings a deeper understanding of their topic to both themselves and their community. Students who are seeking to graduate with honors must complete a fourth passage independently anytime during their high school years.

"Passages at DCIS are the heart and soul of our students' progression to a higher level of being engaged in the world. Passages allow the student the opportunity to develop a deep passion about a subject. The skills and knowledge learned may guide them into adulthood and begin to shape their direction in life after high school."

Beyond the Core

In many schools, the core content areas focus on mathematics, English language arts, science, and social studies and history. In globally focused schools, equal attention is paid to the role arts and world language instruction play in developing students' global competence. This expanded definition of core courses reflects the importance of being a well-rounded individual in a global society. In addition to these areas, there are opportunities for students to find global connections in career and technical courses, health and physical education, and other interdisciplinary studies.

Increased diversity in our schools and communities raises the expectations that students will be able to communicate in multiple languages. Unfortunately, many American schools have not historically put a high priority on language instruction, especially in increasingly tough budgetary times. Only 50 percent of U.S. high school students study a world language, and 70 percent of those simply take one year of introductory Spanish, which is not sufficient to communicate. Moreover, opportunities for students in urban schools to study a world language are often more limited than they are for students in suburban or private schools (Asia Society, 2008). With regard to world language instruction, the United States falls behind most other industrialized nations; for many developed countries, world language instruction starts at the primary level and continues until students are proficient in the target language. While schools in most industrialized nations begin world language instruction in the primary grades and keep at it daily for years until students achieve proficiency, schools in the United States typically offer too little too late and students often do not attain proficiency. Moreover, U.S. schools do not pay attention to languages growing in global significance such as Chinese, Korean, Japanese, and Arabic (Asia Society, 2008).

Success in the 21st century will require students to communicate in multiple languages and with a contextual understanding of other cultures and belief systems. Learning languages goes far beyond the ability to communicate with people from other countries; it involves understanding their culture, beliefs, and practices. Students need opportunities to use their increasing language skills and intercultural knowledge in immersive experiences beyond the world language classroom. Through these experiences, students acquire at least intermediate-level proficiency in both oral and written language communication in their selected world language. In a high-functioning world language classroom, teachers conduct almost all instruction in the target language. Through these experiences, students gain the knowledge and ability to observe and analyze other cultures and use cultural competencies for successful cross-cultural interactions.

Visual and performing arts provide powerful and engaging ways to globalize the curriculum. Appreciating the global influences on contemporary art, music, and film allows students to understand their own culture and the culture of others more deeply. Most communities, including rural communities, offer opportunities for students to engage in the arts at local museums and theaters. The arts provide a unique way to motivate students and develop their curiosity about people who are different than themselves. Providing opportunities to experience live performance or learn alongside local artists, artisans, and musicians deepens students' understanding and appreciation of various cultures.

While the role of all ISSN schools is to assist students in developing the skills and dispositions necessary to succeed in college, we must also acknowledge the fact that some students will pursue a different pathway following high school. Career and technical education pathways allow students to follow areas of interest and in some cases earn technical credentials, certifications, and licenses for work beyond high school. Regardless of the pathway they choose, students in these careers will need to possess high levels of critical-thinking, problem-solving, and collaboration skills.

Travel

The use of technology is one way to bring the world to your students, but nothing can match the experience of bringing your students to the world. Providing opportunities for students to travel, either domestically or internationally, gives them the chance to not only learn about other people but also develop self-confidence and a deeper understanding of themselves. If possible, schools should attempt to provide all students with at least one school-sponsored overnight travel experience during their school career. While these trips can be expensive, schools can engage the community to help support students who cannot afford to travel. Exchange programs and school partnerships can also provide travel opportunities. In addition, schools should help students become aware and take advantage of travel opportunities outside organizations sponsor, such as Rotary International, People to People International, and the American Friends Service Committee.

The goal here is not to travel for travel's sake. In particular, school-sponsored travel should have a direct connection to the curriculum and assist in deepening the student's inquiry into content matter. Learning about water issues in a foreign country brings home the concepts taught in environmental science class. Visiting a mosque can deepen the appreciation of world religions taught in advanced placement world history. Visiting other countries allows students to reflect on their own culture, values, and beliefs. For many students, traveling outside their country causes an awakening, as they realize the luxuries and opportunities they have compared to less industrialized nations. For many, it is also the first time they realize that America is not the first or best at everything in the world. In most cases, their worldview, both locally and globally, begins to expand. However, it isn't always necessary to leave the United States to have this kind of learning experience. Students who live in rural communities or urban settings have often never been outside their town or city limits. In fact, there are students living in New York City, one of the most diverse cities in the world, who have never even been to another borough, where life looks different than where they call home.

SCHOOL SPOTLIGHT: ACADEMY FOR GLOBAL STUDIES AT AUSTIN HIGH SCHOOL, AUSTIN, TEXAS

Many schools in the United States take their students to visit Washington, DC. Teachers at the Academy for Global Studies (AGS) at Austin High School decided to turn a typical class trip into a powerful learning experience beyond simply seeing the sites. Modeled after a similar project of the International School of the Americas in San Antonio, the AGS teachers' interdisciplinary project asked students to work in teams to research a specific global topic related to the United Nations Millennium Development Goals or the Universal Declaration of Human Rights. Once in teams, students developed overarching questions to help them explore their topic more deeply and to guide their inquiry. Research took place prior to the trip but also was meant to continue while in Washington.

Prior to departure, teachers required each team to contact organizations the students felt would assist them in addressing their issue. They had to display diplomatic and superior communication skills to secure appointments at places such as embassies, U.S. governmental offices, and nongovernmental organizations (NGOs). Each team member played a certain role once the travel teams arrived in DC. The project required the team to investigate the topic from multiple perspectives, think about what stance it would take in addressing the problem, and decide how best to communicate its findings to a broad audience.

Upon returning home, teams made public presentations and defended their findings to a panel composed of their teachers and community members. One team, for example, studied human trafficking and asked a local member of the border patrol to serve on the panel to ensure that their findings and assertions were correct. The project addressed standards in science, English language arts, and social studies, demonstrating how travel and inquiry can provide powerful and meaningful ways to address curriculum demands.

Other School Structures

In my experience, schools focusing on global competence make a concerted effort to foster the development of adult and student relationships to promote students' personal, academic, and social growth. This can be accomplished through the development of formal structures, such as courses, electives, clubs, or extracurricular activities that promote global competence. For example, some schools have turned Model United Nations, typically seen as an after-school club, into an actual course. Other schools have revamped existing courses to provide a more global focus, such as International Economics and Business, or have broken courses like world history into smaller minicourses such as Religions of the World, Conflict Throughout History, and Cultural Studies.

SCHOOL SPOTLIGHT: INTERNATIONAL STUDIES LEARNING CENTER, SOUTH GATE, CALIFORNIA

Imagine a time before computers, television, and phones, when we communicated only by talking with each other face to face. We signaled the beginning of our time together with a song or a statement. We remembered our traditions and discovered our values. We shared our strengths and acknowledged our challenges. We made decisions, explored conflicts, and shared our dreams. We told our stories. Sometimes we passed a talking piece from person to person, so the speaker was the center of attention. Finally, we signaled the closing of our time together with songs, silence, or an acknowledgment of what had been done and what remained.

Joe Provisor, director of the Ojai Foundation's Council in Schools program, helps teachers and students at the International Studies Learning Center (ISLC) share their innermost thoughts and ideas while building community using the council process. Based on indigenous, worldwide "cultural dialogical" practices, including Native American traditions, council is a formal, structured process that includes sitting in a circle and passing a "talking piece" in response to a prompt from the facilitator. In the classroom, teachers and students might develop their own intentions (guidelines) or use the "four intentions" of council, as developed by students and facilitators associated with the Ojai Foundation:

- To listen from the heart: practicing the "art of receptivity," suspending judgment, reaction, and opinion

- To speak from the heart and with the heart: learning to "speak into the listening"

- To speak spontaneously without planning and only when holding a "talking piece."

- To "keep it lean" or get to the "heart of the matter" so everyone has time with the talking piece. (Ojai Foundation Council in Schools, n.d.)

LEADER ACTION STEPS

- Assist teachers in identifying strategic points in the curriculum to embed global issues and go deeper with performance-based assessments.

- Create a schoolwide curriculum map that highlights when and how teachers will teach the different domains of global competence.

- Provide professional development to teachers to assist them in creating a more student-centered classroom that focuses on authentic learning experiences.

- Promote an interdisciplinary, project-based learning culture in which students work collaboratively with peers locally and globally.

- Evaluate the different courses and structures in your school for which you can adopt or create a global focus.

- Consider ways (other than test scores) to demonstrate and celebrate student learning, such as portfolio assessment, student-led parent conferences, or celebration of learning nights.

- Identify ways to create learning experiences outside the school walls through community-based projects, student travel, or internships.

Advisory

Advisory serves as a home base for students and allows them to discuss issues pertaining to their schoolwork or personal life or to engage in longer-term projects with their advisory teacher. Often these groups stay together and meet with the same advisory to create a safe, family-like atmosphere. This structure allows for mentoring, advisement, and support on things like student portfolios, long-term group projects, and personal goal setting. To keep the global focus, some advisories adopt global themes or refer to themselves as *embassies*. Often, this is the place where current events and timely global issues find their way into the curriculum and provide a place for discussion among students. The ultimate goal of this structure is to ensure that there are multiple adults in the school who know and care about the students and who can be readily accessible as needed. The advisory provides students with opportunities to develop and express themselves on personal, academic, schoolwide, and international issues.

One specific activity that is sometimes conducted in advisory is called *councils*. Schools often use the council process in their advisory program once a week, usually on Fridays. Council provides students with a safe, supportive environment to raise problems, concerns, and questions about their lives, school, and the world around them. Just as important, it has taught students how to listen to others, show respect for different opinions, and develop their voice. This process has served to give all students and teachers in a school a voice and a way to learn about and from each other. Time can range from twenty minutes to an entire class period one or more times a week. Besides training the staff to run councils, students in each advisory can be trained to lead or colead the process as well.

Strategy Four: Leverage Technology

Unlike any other time in history, the 21st century allows us access to information at the click of a button. While the immediate access to a wealth of knowledge is empowering, understanding how to find relevant and accurate information, make sense of that information, and use it in appropriate ways have created new challenges for 21st century students. The advent of mobile computing devices, including cell phones, video cameras, and iPads, has forever changed the landscape of classrooms around the world. The digital age has made "going global" instant, cheaper, and more personal. The question is, How will schools adapt to these rapidly changing innovations? The truth is that our students are already doing it.

Advances in technology change the way students learn and communicate about that learning. For instance, students asked to meet the demand of investigating the world now have access to endless information and resources at their fingertips. With the rise in mobile technologies, including smart phones, students have the ability to access information quicker and more conveniently than at any other time in history. However, helping students become discerning consumers of that knowledge requires refined skills. It has now become vitally important for students to be critical consumers of information, to understand where the information comes from, why it was created in the format it's in, and what potential issues exist involving accuracy.

The Internet provides students with the opportunity to interact with others who hold different perspectives on a number of issues, both local and global. By experiencing different perspectives, students test their own understanding of issues and personal beliefs. Expressing ideas and communicating with a global audience have become tremendously easier as well. Students can now share their learning, opinions, and understanding of world events through blogs, wikis, and social networking tools like Facebook and Twitter. This creates a powerful shift for students from being the *consumers* of information to the *creators* of information. With this immediacy of sharing ideas and information comes certain responsibilities and the need to understand the perspectives of others; knowing how to share information ethically is more important for students than ever before.

An easy area in which students can engage with technology is the fourth domain of global competence—take action. Students are able to access any number of social and political movements. The current generation have developed a strong voice and an interest in influencing the world around them. One very tangible international example is the Arab Spring of 2010 (The Telegraph, 2011), which saw youth in several Middle Eastern countries launch protests and demand reforms in their countries. These protests and calls to action began largely through the use of social media. Learning about problems in faraway countries may have been part of the curriculum before, but 21st century technology allows students to actually connect with those problems, serve as actors, and do something about them. Alongside these authentic, real-world opportunities, the mundane and traditional tasks we ask students to do in many traditional classrooms pale in significance. It is hard for students to get excited about writing a book report in one classroom when down the hall they've been coordinating efforts with relief workers in Africa to install a well to provide drinking water to an entire village. And you must excuse students who don't get excited about yet another teacher-directed lesson when in another classroom they were just creating a budget and implementation plan for a community service project and getting estimates from vendors online. Technology has redefined the type of work we must ask our students to produce and changed the definition of the classroom.

Increasingly, teachers too are taking advantage of technology to engage with other educators from around the world. For example, teachers and administrators utilize the ISSN Ning (issnny.ning.com)—a closed, online community in which the sharing of resources, online chats, and group conversations allow colleagues to focus on pertinent topics and timely articles and where users post videos related to global education. This type of professional development extends learning beyond the faculty room and allows teachers from different geographic regions to collaborate and work toward a common goal. These approaches model the concept of *anytime, anywhere* learning that we hope to extend to our students.

Educators who are just getting their feet wet in the global education pool should investigate the Global Education Conference (www.globaleducationconference .com) each November. Since 2007, founders Lucy Gray and Steve Hargadon have created a truly amazing interactive global conference that has served students, educators, and organizations committed to the notion of global education at all levels. The around-the-clock conference leads to education-related connections around the globe and further develops cultural awareness and diversity for all who participate. Thousands of practitioners from a variety of fields convene online for a week to share their expertise, ideas, and solutions to complex world problems. For educators just starting out, this free resource provides great models and potential projects to bring back to the classroom. Just as importantly, it currently serves as the largest virtual community discussing and promoting global education.

CLASSROOM-TO-CLASSROOM CONNECTIONS

One meaningful way to engage students in the use of technology is through formal classroom connections. Through virtual, project-based learning experiences, students collaborate with students in other locations (domestically or internationally) to learn about world issues and each other. The key is to engage students in learning *with* their international peers instead of *about* them. Following are several resources that can help you connect your students.

- **iEARN:** The International Education and Resource Network (iEARN) "is a nonprofit organization made up of over 30,000 schools and youth organizations in more than 130 countries. iEARN empowers teachers and young people to work together online using the Internet and other new communications technologies. Over 2,000,000 students each day are engaged in collaborative project work worldwide" (iEARN, n.d.).

- **ePals:** ePals "offers elementary and secondary school administrators, teachers, students, and parents worldwide a safe and secure platform for building educational communities, providing quality digital content and facilitating collaboration for effective 21st century learning" (ePals, 2013).

- **UClass:** UClass.org is a global lesson-plan exchange that allows teachers to share high-quality lessons, thereby enabling students to collaborate with other students around the world who are learning the same lesson. UClass taps into the global wealth of experience and knowledge by gathering, sharing, and crowd-sourcing planning (UClass.org, n.d.).

- **Flat Classroom Project:** "The Flat Classroom Project is a global collaborative project that joins together middle and senior high

Continued →

school students" (Flat Classroom Project, n.d.). The project allows schools that "embrace a holistic and constructivist educational approach to work collaboratively" through educational networking platforms with others around the world in order to create students who are competitive and globally minded (Flat Classroom Project, n.d.).

- **Challenge 20/20:** Organized by the National Association of Independent Schools (2013), "Challenge 20/20 is an Internet-based program that pairs classes at any grade level (K–12) from schools in the U.S. with their counterparts in other countries; together, teams of two or three schools find local solutions to one of twenty global problems."

School leaders must leverage the use of technology in these meaningful ways to engage students and faculty. Unfortunately, far too many schools and districts still lock down the use of technology for fear that students will use the tools for ill. My own view is that students will use technology appropriately only when schools offer opportunities to use that technology ethically and responsibly and provide clear expectations. Campuses moving toward BYOD and expecting teachers and students to engage in an online space such as a blog, wiki, or Moodle will better prepare students for the world they live in.

LEADER ACTION STEPS

- Prioritize the use of technology as a means to promote global competence for adults and students.
- Model the use of technology through your own use of a blog or social media application.
- Encourage student participation in online projects and competition.
- Support teachers' attempts to engage with educators throughout the world to improve their practice by improving the technology infrastructure in the school and opening the campus for more access.

Strategy Five: Grow Global Leaders

Schools that begin down the path of globalization often do so behind the leadership of a principal or administrator, whose position allows him or her to help set the vision, create some of the structures necessary to do the actual work, and serve as a conduit to the community. For the work to persist long-term, it is imperative to utilize a shared or distributive leadership model. While one principal or teacher can make a significant difference in a school, the power of many individuals working toward a common goal is obvious. All too often, these types of school innovations or reforms end abruptly with a change in leadership. Developing intentional ways to invest teachers, students, and community members ensures that the focus on global competence becomes part of the school's DNA. It says, "It's just the way we do business here."

Successful globally focused schools require teachers to be organized into high-performing, instructionally focused teams that have common planning time within the instructional day. Time for grade-level or discipline-specific teams to meet is critical in order for them to improve curriculum, instruction, and assessment. It is during this time that they can explore how to integrate global content and perspectives while developing plans to meet the individual students' or group needs. Teams engage in reflective processes to enhance the use of planning time. When possible, vertical planning and subject-matter discussions also take place during this time.

Teams create decision-making structures to support the efficient functioning of the school and ensure effective involvement of stakeholders from the community. For example, action teams composed of teachers, students, and community members can focus on key aspects of the school design, represent different perspectives, and provide the hands necessary to make change. The term *action teams* is purposeful; it indicates that a team meets for a purpose, makes decisions to move toward that action, and can theoretically be disbanded or reconvene around a new action once it has met the goal. Especially in small schools, teachers wear many hats, but they are also skeptical and tired of myriad meetings that do not result in action. Repurposing existing teams or committees will communicate new priorities and intentionality.

To help students develop global competence, faculty members too must be able to grow in this area. By working collaboratively and engaging in job-embedded, meaningful professional development, the collective capacity of the staff will grow (Croft, Coggshall, Dolan, Powers, & Killion, 2010). The faculty and administration must develop and model, over time, a school climate in which sharing, risk taking, and curiosity are norms. Globally focused schools must encourage and provide support for faculty travel, language learning, and other experiences that will further develop their own global competence.

Educators who participate on learning teams within their school can collaborate and learn from others. The development of local, national, and international partnerships allows teachers to harness the collective knowledge of the profession. Using structures such as Critical Friends Groups (www.nsrfharmony.org/faq.html), lesson study, practitioner research, and peer observations provide various ways teachers can learn from and with one another. Selecting teachers to help lead some of these practices ensures that teacher leadership and capacity are spread among the faculty and not concentrated in the school administration. The use of international book clubs, for example, is a fun and affordable way to expand teachers' horizons, build a common vocabulary, and deepen thinking on issues and topics relevant to society.

Faculties in these settings focus on evidence of student learning in an effort to improve teaching and learning. For example, a major component of the Graduation Performance System is the collaborative assessment of student work. In these protocols, teachers analyze student work in an effort to find evidence of student learning measured against a rubric. This practice allows teachers to check their expectations of student learning against one another and find ways to provide students with rich feedback to improve their work. It also allows teachers to reflect on their role in students' learning and what to do differently next time. Active learner engagement, clear application to the classroom, and reflections on its effectiveness characterize professional development in these schools.

Of course, for this type of inquiry approach to take place, faculty members must have time and resources, while also having access to other relevant professional learning such as coursework, conferences, and school study tours. Providing teachers with frequent opportunities for reflection and a rich body of resources related to globalizing their classroom will increase the likelihood that those practices will be reflected in their instruction.

Sustaining a global focus in your school requires more than adults being on board. As mentioned previously, students should also play a role in the decision making and planning process for the school. For example, students can play a role in the development of curriculum, assessment, and overall school governance. This creates more buy-in from students and motivates them to be active participants in the school. A school that possesses a strong student voice makes decisions based more on the needs of its students than the needs of the adults.

LEADER ACTION STEPS

- Create time for faculty members to collaborate and develop global learning experiences for students.
- Distribute leadership and responsibility among all staff members to support long-term sustainability.
- Utilize high-quality professional development that differentiates the needs of adults.
- Formally involve students in helping to inform what is taught and how the school operates.

Strategy Six: Create Global Partnerships

Many of the strategies and approaches shared in this chapter do not necessarily require outside support or additional funding. Some initiatives, however, such as travel, internships, and providing real-world experiences, may permit opportunities for partnerships with entities outside the school. Partnerships with internationally oriented academic, business, and community organizations can assist in identifying financial resources and opportunities for students. Creating partnerships within the community is a key strategy for globalizing your school.

These community partner organizations serve as advocates for the school in the local community and beyond. In addition, they provide key resources for both students and adults. For example, partnerships with local higher education institutions may allow for dual enrollment or credit-bearing courses for students, as well as professional development opportunities for adults. Local colleges and universities also provide access to international students and expert faculty on a variety of world topics and help foster the college-going culture we hope to offer all globally competent students.

Schools can establish formal partnerships with any number of organizations— museums, international organizations or institutions, humanitarian organizations, labor groups, and volunteer organizations. Increasingly, schools are also fostering partnerships with schools in other places around the globe. Through organizations such as Sister Cities International and World Affairs Councils of America and websites like ePals, teachers are able to establish relationships with schools and colleagues in other countries. These relationships enable teachers to develop projects and learning experiences that connect students of different cultures and backgrounds.

LEADER ACTION STEPS

- Survey the local community to identify any organizations or businesses (including restaurants) that have an international focus or connection.
- Research grant and program opportunities at the state, national, and international levels to support your efforts.
- Invite international guests and delegations from different countries to visit your school and interact with students.

Conclusion

It is my hope that the six strategies presented in this chapter will help guide your thinking about promoting a schoolwide approach to global competence. Two final points are necessary to stress. First, while a schoolwide approach may allow for a deeper commitment and path to global competence, it is not the only way this can occur. If you are a teacher reading this chapter, you can and should think about how these principles might play out in your classroom, regardless of your school's disposition and interest in this work. In other words, creating globally focused learning experiences can happen one classroom at a time. Schools attempting to transform the teaching and learning within their school are more apt to be successful when focusing as an entire community, but over time, individual teachers can find ways to link their efforts together; by making interdisciplinary connections and opening their classrooms up to the world, they will empower their students to make richer connections and hold on to the learning longer.

Secondly, the strategies do not need to be done in a certain order or all at once. Furthermore, because of the needs of the community, financial limitations, or competing initiatives, not all pieces will work exactly as written for every setting. With that said, schools such as the ones in the ISSN serve as an example that this type of learning can be successful in all types of communities and with diverse groups of students. Whether you are starting a new school or hoping to transform one that has an existing faculty, culture, and way of doing business, it is critical to be purposeful about how to implement the changes over time. Learning from other examples, whether domestically or internationally, is a valuable step in making those decisions and underscoring the importance of networking. By learning *from* and *with* the world, your school will be better prepared to assist young people to succeed in the 21st century.

References and Resources

Ambassador School of Global Leadership. (n.d.). *Beliefs.* Accessed at http://
asgl-lausd-ca.schoolloop.com/beliefs on September 10, 2013.

Asia Society. (2008). *Going global: Preparing our students for an interconnected world.*
New York: Author.

Asia Society. (2012a). *International Studies Schools Network: A graduate profile for the
21st century.* Accessed at http://asiasociety.org/education/international-studies
-schools-network/graduate-profile-21st-century on May 14, 2012.

Asia Society. (2013a). *Education.* Accessed at www.asiasociety.org/education on July
18, 2013.

Asia Society. (2012b). *International Studies Schools Network: Teacher profile—Qualities
of a 21st century teacher.* Accessed at http://asiasociety.org/education/international
-studies-schools-network/teacher-profile on May 14, 2012.

Asia Society. (2012c). *SAGE questions and strategies.* Accessed at www.issnny.ning.com
/page/sage-overview on April 20, 2013.

Asia Society. (2013d). *Global competence: Prepare youth to engage with the world.*
Accessed at http://asiasociety.org/education/partnership-global-learning/making
-case/global-competence-prepare-youth-engage-world on September 10, 2013.

Committee for Economic Development. (2006). *Education for global leadership: The
importance of international studies and foreign language education for U.S. economic
and national security.* Washington, DC: Author. Accessed at www.ced.org/pdf
/Education-for-Global-Leadership.pdf on April 20, 2013.

Croft, A., Coggshall, J., Dolan, M., Powers, E., & Killion, J. (2010). *Job-embedded
professional development: What it is, who is responsible, and how to get it done well.*
Accessed at www.learningforward.org/docs/pdf/jobembeddedpdbrief
.pdf?sfvrsn=0 on September 27, 2013.

Denver Center for International Studies at Montbello. (n.d.). *About.* Accessed at
www.dcismontbello.org/about on September 10, 2013.

Diamond, J. (1999). *Guns, germs, and steel: The fates of human societies.* New York:
W.W. Norton & Company, Inc.

Dresser, N. (2005). *Multicultural manners: Essential rules of etiquette for the 21st
century.* Hoboken, NJ: John Wiley & Sons.

EdSteps. (n.d.). *Global competence.* Accessed at www.edsteps.org/CCSSO/Manage
Content.aspx?system_name=I5nka44NofDD3IY38QBonx+Crwfdw
+uF&selected_system_name=DRkDdjiObdU= on September 10, 2013.

ePals. (2013). *About us.* Accessed at www.corp.epals.com/about-us.php on May 1, 2013.

Flat Classroom Project. (n.d.). *About: What is the Flat Classroom Project?* Accessed at www.flatclassroomproject.org/About on May 15, 2013.

Friedman, T. L. (2005). *The world is flat: A brief history of the twenty-first century.* New York: Farrar, Straus, and Giroux.

iEARN. (n.d.). *About.* Accessed at http://iearn.org/about on May 1, 2013.

Jacobs, H. H. (Ed.). (2014). *Mastering global literacy.* Bloomington, IN: Solution Tree Press.

Mansilla, V. B., & Jackson, T. (2011). *Educating for global competence: Preparing our youth to engage the world.* New York: Asia Society.

Mansilla, & V. B. Jackson, A. W. (2014). Educating for global competence: Redefining learning for an interconnected world. In H. H. Jacobs (Ed.), *Mastering global literacy* (pp. 5–29). Bloomington, IN: Solution Tree Press.

National Association of Independent Schools. (2013, March 27). *Challenge 20/20.* Accessed at www.nais.org/Articles/Pages/Challenge-20-20.aspx on May 1, 2013.

Reimers, F. M. (2009). Leading for global competency. *Educational Leadership, 67*(1). Accessed at www.ascd.org/publications/educational-leadership/sept09/vol67/num01/Leading-for-Global-Competency.aspx on February 12, 2013.

Ojai Foundation Council in Schools. (n.d.) *About CIS—What is Council?* Accessed at http://cis.ojaifoundation.org/about-cis/what-council on September 10, 2013.

The Telegraph. (2011, October). Arab Spring: Timeline of the African and Middle East rebellions. Accessed at www.telegraph.co.uk/news/worldnews/africa andindianocean/libya/8839143/Arab-Spring-timeline-of-the-African-and-Middle -East-rebellions.html on September 10, 2013.

Wiggins, G., & McTighe, J. (2005). *Understanding by design* (2nd ed.). Alexandria, VA: American Society for Curriculum Development.

World Savvy. (2012, July 26). *World Savvy: Global competency research results.* Accessed at http://worldsavvy.org/assets/documents/uploads/Final_WS_Market_Research _Study_Aug_2012.pdf on February 10, 2013.

Index

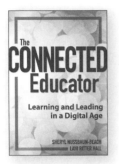

The Connected Educator
Sheryl Nussbaum-Beach and Lani Ritter Hall
Create a connected learning community through social media and rediscover the power of being a learner first. The authors show you how to take advantage of technology to collaborate with other educators and deepen the learning of your students.
BKF478

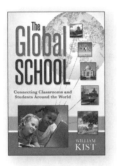

The Global School
By William Kist
Prepare students for an increasingly flat world where diverse people from divergent cultures learn and work together rather than in isolation. Learn specific steps to globalize your classroom and encourage higher-order thinking, all wrapped in a 21st century skills framework.
BKF570

21st Century Skills
Edited by James A. Bellanca and Ron Brandt
Examine the Framework for 21st Century Learning from the Partnership for 21st Century Skills as a way to re-envision learning in a rapidly evolving global and technological world. Learn why these skills are necessary, which are most important, and how to best help schools include them.
BKF389

Bringing Innovation to School
By Suzie Boss
Activate your students' creativity and problem-solving potential with breakthrough learning projects. Across all grades and content areas, student-driven, collaborative projects will teach students how to generate innovative ideas and then put them into action.
BKF546

Solution Tree | Press
a division of
Solution Tree

Visit solution-tree.com or call 800.733.6786 to order.

Wait! Your professional development journey doesn't have to end with the last pages of this book.

We realize improving student learning doesn't happen overnight. And your school or district shouldn't be left to puzzle out all the details of this process alone.

No matter where you are on the journey, we're committed to helping you get to the next stage.

Take advantage of everything from **custom workshops** to **keynote presentations** and **interactive web and video conferencing**. We can even help you develop an action plan tailored to fit your specific needs.

Let's get the conversation started.

Call 888.763.9045 today.

 solution-tree.com